PUT YOUR
NAME ON IT:

....

P9-BYS-601

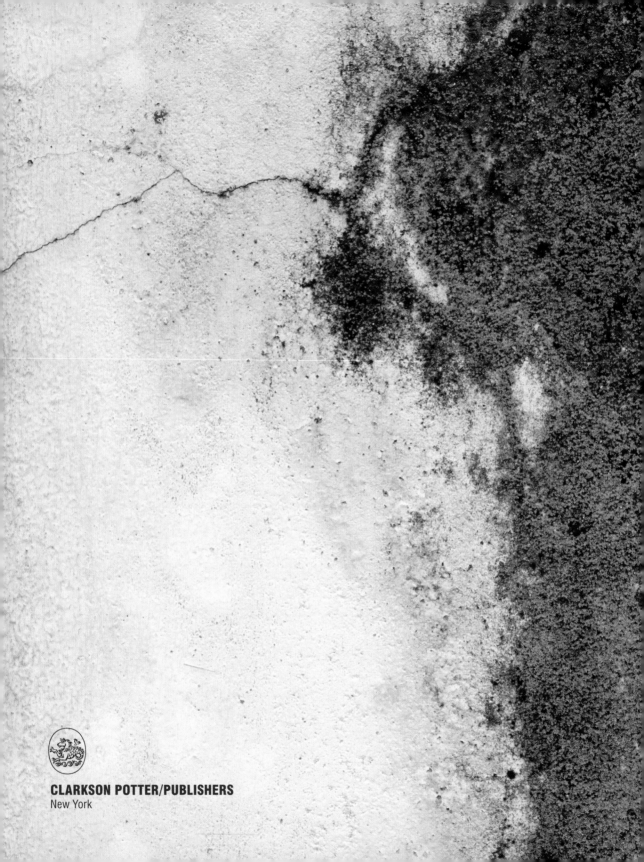

CLARKSON POTTER/PUBLISHERS
New York

COOK LIKE A LOCAL

THE
PORTLANDIA
COOKBOOK

FRED ARMISEN
AND
CARRIE BROWNSTEIN
WITH JONATHAN KRISEL

PHOTOGRAPHS BY EVAN SUNG

www.crownpublishing.com
www.clarksonpotter.com

CLARKSON POTTER is a trademark and POTTER with colophon
is a registered trademark of Random House LLC.

"Portlandia" and its related characters and trademarks are property of
Broadway Video Entertainment, Inc.

Library of Congress Cataloging-in-Publication Data
Armisen, Fred, 1966–
  The Portlandia cookbook : cook like a local / Fred Armisen and
Carrie Brownstein, with Jonathan Krisel ; photographs by Evan Sung.
      pages cm
  Includes index.
  1. Cooking, American—Pacific Northwest style. 2. Cooking—
Oregon—Portland. 3. Local foods—Oregon—Portland. I. Brownstein,
Carrie, 1974– II. Krisel, Jonathan. III. Title.
  TX715.2.P32A82 2014
  641.59795'49—dc23

                        2014008650

ISBN 978-0-8041-8610-0
eBook ISBN 978-0-8041-8611-7

Printed in China

Text by Alice Mathias

Recipes by Grace Parisi

Book design by Rae Ann Spitzenberger

Cover design by Jim Massey and Rae Ann Spitzenberger

Front cover photography by Evan Sung

Back cover: iStock © Creativeye99 (wood); martijnmulder (tape);
Shutterstock © serazetdinov (paper); © Yurkaimmortal (skyline);
Evan Sung (bark, burger, Candace and Toni); IFC (Bryce & Lisa)

For additional photography credits, and for illustration credits,
see page 172.

10 9 8 7 6 5

First Edition

DISCLAIMER

THE PORTLAND ALLERGY COUNCIL: "NO NEED TO BE RASH"

The following book has been reviewed and approved by the Portland Allergy Council. It has received a grade of "PROCEED WITH CAUTION, BUT OVERALL GOOD COOKBOOK." Ingredient substitutions for a variety of allergies have been registered in the Allergy Council Archives at Portland City Hall. They can be retrieved by contacting our staff by phone during office hours: Tuesday–Friday (9:00 a.m.–5:30 p.m.); Saturdays (10:00 a.m.–3:00 p.m.). Closed Sundays and Mondays. Please be advised that due to a high volume of allergy-related calls you may be immediately directed to our voice-mail box. We are okay with checking voice mail and will not act like we never saw your message. It's actually a good way to reach us. Thank you in advance for leaving us a voice mail.

CONTENTS

CONTRIBUTORS

This book is a collection of recipes from all over Portland. Contributors range from professional chefs to people who made something really great at home one time. Each recipe has been vetted by The Portland Society of Food Hobbyists, who all agreed everything tastes good.

KATH & DAVE

Have all of the kitchen gear required for a 100% authentic dish.

NINA & LANCE

Share a love for cacao, birthday tapas, and each other.

SPYKE

The intense bicycle-rights advocate challenges you to think about what you're eating.

BRYCE & LISA

Can pickle that.

MARCO

The 911 Beets Hotline operator shares a recipe for the most frequently reported case of beet-related trauma.

BRENDAN & MICHELLE

Finally figured out what to do with the durian from their CSA box!!!

MR. MAYOR

Our city's beloved leader knows a top-secret spot for the best brunch in town.

THE RATS

Foodies and frequenters of Portland's finest garbage cans.

GUTTERPUNKS

Know how to eat well for one dollar. Do you have a dollar?

ELLEN

Adult babysitter. Shares the recipe for the #1 best mac and cheese in the world, according to Doug.

GARMIN
A little guy with
a big appetite.

JOHNNY
A waiter at SoCal's
Around the World
in 80 Plates.

ROCKSTAR
CHEFS
Professional chefs
who photograph
really well.

DOUG & CLAIRE
Have mastered
the TV dinner after
experimenting with
many, many TV
dinners.

PETER &
NANCE
Committed to
conscious eating.
Their recipe requires
a locally sourced
chicken.

STU & DONALD
Owners and
operators of
Portland's widely
unknown food cart,
Stu's Stews.

MALCOLM
& KRIS
Their organic vegan
recipe requires
immediate access
to a fart patio.

ALEXANDRA
Fred and Carrie's
one-time roommate
shares her favorite
recipe for lasagna
with Cheez Whiz
frosting.

MARTY
Has fresh ideas
for the best
use of America's
#1 vegetable.
(Celery, of course.)

JOAQUIN
Shares a nutritious
smoothie recipe that
will support a healthy
workout routine.

TONI &
CANDACE
Owners and operators
of Women and Women
First bookstore.
Recipes intended for
women ONLY.

ALIKI
A humble farmer.

INTRODUCTION

Portland, Oregon, is a food town. We owe this reputation to the quality of local ingredients, the widespread creativity of our chefs—and the fact that the City of Portland needed to come up with a reputation and was like: no city has taken "food town" yet?! Let's *definitely* go with "food town"!

The food in Portland often has some kind of compelling story behind it. Like the story of where the ingredients were foraged from. Or how the meal has been cooked by wood-fired oven in a Luddite kitchen—with no involvement of technology at all. Or maybe technology is super-involved. You can design your own doughnut with a videogame controller. Or what you think is ice cream turns out to be steak and it's somehow actually good. Often people here *make* the *ingredients* they use to make things. They tell you the story of how they learned to brew their own vinegar. They describe the whole process of brewing vinegar and you don't really follow, but it is *very* impressive that they made vinegar. They have even started packaging it in interesting, reappropriated old bottles with cute, hand-drawn labels. If all goes well with this stuff they're bottling at home, they have this idea to open a vinegar brewery. It would be like a fun beer garden, but for vinegar. There are "drinking vinegars" that you can just pour in a pint glass and drink like a normal drink. It can even be a little alcoholic if you're looking to party. Chocolate vinegar exists. You can freeze vinegar like a popsicle and it's only *kind of* bad. . . . That's just the beginning of how interesting vinegar can be, believe us. (Some stories are longer than others.)

The recipes in this cookbook come from all over town. Each is accompanied by a note from the contributor—some of whom are professional chefs, and others just cook for fun with family and friends at home. The book includes recipes from local restaurants, coffee shops, bed and breakfasts, and farms. And Mr. Mayor finally dishes on the secret to his Jamaican Jerk Chicken!

Okay, that's probably enough explaining what the book is going to be like. . . . We won't keep you from your meal any longer. Have fun in the kitchen!

—FRED AND CARRIE

PORTLAND
Food Map

NORTHEAST PORTLAND
1. Fisherman's Porch
2. Stu's Stews Featuring Donald
3. The Knot Store
4. NE Portland Community Garden
5. Thai Restaurant Disguised as Bridgetown Weekly
6. The MODA Center—Home of the Annual Prairie Home Companion Tailgate
7. Portland Community College Dining Hall (Dollar Discount with ID)
8. Peter and Nance's B&B, The Quilted Tea Kettle Inn
9. Women and Women First
10. Tavin's Pub, Home of the "Burn Your Face Off Margarita"

SOUTHEAST PORTLAND
11. 1890s Butcherarium
12. Organic Vegan Restaurant (and Fart Patio!)
13. Peter's Favorite Italian Joint
14. The Dumpster Behind Jewel of India
15. Community Supported Agriculture Shipping Center
16. Bryce and Lisa's Chicken Coop
17. Bryce and Lisa's Pickle Co-op
18. Gahvin's Recording Studio
19. Underground Meeting Place, The Society of Baristas of Portland, Oregon

NORTHWEST PORTLAND
20. Nina's Favorite Tapas Restaurant
21. Onetime Home of Nicholas's Greek Restaurant
22. Taco Town (Dollar Taco Tuesday)
23. McGinnis Pub (Dollar Beer, 1–4 p.m.)
24. Pizza Face (Dollar Meal Monday)
25. The Doughnut Hole (Dollar Day-Old Doughnuts)
26. Mom's House
27. Smoothie Jam

SOUTHWEST PORTLAND
28. Mr. Mayor's Café Y2K
29. Artisanal Movie Theater
30. The Portland Allergy Council at City Hall
31. 911-Beets Call Center
32. The Portland Milk Advisory Board Research Labs

OUTSIDE PORTLAND
33. Aliki Farms

205

EAST

NOTE ON AUTHENTICITY AND GETTING THE GEAR

BY KATH AND DAVE

So you're a serious chef, apparently. *Un étudiant de cuisine.* A culinary *tour de force de la comida* (Note: French and Spanish). From our travels both abroad and in our homeland, we've learned one thing about The Great Chefs of Our Time. The Great Chefs all abide by one fundamental culinary order: Having the Right Tools.

CRUCIAL TOOLS FOR THE AUTHENTIC KITCHEN INCLUDE:

* Passport
* Passport holder *(neck strap recommended to wear underneath vest for security)*
* Vest
* Backup vest
* Alternate form of photo ID *(keep separate from passport in second on-body ID holder)*
* Dave recommends travel pillow, but Kath says: "Optional."
* Chopsticks *(Kath is laughing because it's so obvious)*
* Granola bars *(emergency)*
* Two 3- to 4-pound rocks, medium-hard
* Grass mat *(general straining needs)*
* Forks: American, Scandinavian, Italian spaghetti fork, fondue fork, spork encouraged *(knorks are for dorks)** *(*Joke by Dave)*

  WARNING: <u>Be aware of American style of fork etiquette vs. European style, in which fork tines curve down when eating. We're gently reminding you. We're aware you already know this. Who wouldn't know this? Hopefully not you.</u>

* Fishing pole
* Fishing net
* Traps, variety
* Swiss Army knife *(recommended for Swiss recipes only—i.e., chopping cubes of cheese for melting into fondue; also okay for opening bottles of Swiss wine; okay to open Swiss regional wines with Army knife, but not recommended for Spanish, Oregon wines, etc., as method of cork removal is proven to affect quality of taste)** *(*Proven by Dave)*
* Thermometer
* Barometer
* Potato chip grabber
* Blender
* Scooper
* Melter
* Hot towels *(rolled up in the heated hot towel box)*
* Plenty of sponges
* Shopping cart *(better to just have your own because of germs, etc.)*
* Le Creuset Signature Cast Iron 2-Quart Soleil Round French Oven
* Candles *(romance)*. Kath says: "Optional."

TO KEEP IT *MUY AUTÉNTICO* . . . TO MAINTAIN THE TRUE SPIRIT OF A DISH'S INTENTION, IT IS *CRUCIAL* TO HAVE THE TOOLS. The original tools. Don't even bother if you don't have the tools. You're making a *mole* sauce in some stainless steel pot you bought at the store one time? This is Dave and I'm laughing out loud. A pot on some stove in your second-floor apartment kitchen? Dave says, "Don't bother," and Kath is nodding her head in a way that means: "Agree with Dave: Do Not Bother."

Do you even know how *mole* sauce is made? On the ground. Not to mention outside. Outside and on the ground.

AUTHENTICALLY MADE *MOLE* REQUIRES:

* ★ **Two 3–4 pound rocks, medium-hard**
* ★ **Sundial**
* ★ ***Camatillo* wood fire (translation: "Mexican Kingwood"), medium-hot fire temperature**
* ★ **The ground (Dirt preferred. Sand okay. Grass is a "no.")**
* ★ **Wooden spoon (Note: *Chechen* wood preferred for spoon wood—erratic grain pattern ideal for mixing. Leftover *Camatillo* wood from the fire is a "Don't bother even thinking about it." *Camatillo* is a fire wood. This is the spoon wood section, and we hope you are paying attention to the difference.)**
* ★ **Le Creuset Signature Cast Iron 2-Quart Soleil Round French Oven. Worth the price, hands down. We've purchased thousands of pots and trust us: what you're paying for here is the authenticity. (Note: We tried making our own cast iron pot. It's a "Don't bother.")**
* ★ **Tongs**
* ★ ***Mole* sauce ingredients**

SO YOU'VE GOT THE TOOLS. You're a little bit thinking you're a whiz now, huh? Not so fast. You want an authentic *mole* sauce? Go to Mexico and make it there. The water and air are different.

For emergencies when we're dying for Kath and Dave's *mole* and we can't get to Mexico in time, we keep handblown glass bottles of Mexican water in our basement water cellar. In fact, our cellar houses a variety of Mexican waters—Aztec and Yucatan Water . . . water sourced from *Puebla.* We use different waters, depending on what regional *mole* we're making. Maybe we go source it from *Oaxaca.* For our extra-spicy *mole*, we've bottled the early morning precipitation from the treetops of *Tabasco* (which is an *actual place*, if you didn't know. *Southeast Mexico,* come on!).

We're talking about commitment to authenticity, which is the #1 quality of a chef. And like we said, if you don't have the water: "Do Not Bother." We won't eat it! Maybe you have some jokey friend you can easily confuse into thinking you made a *mole* in one afternoon on some stove you plugged into the wall. Having ol' Kath and Dave over for dinner? Ha ha. We won't be there. We won't even show up, because we know your *mole* is preposterous. The fact that we're even having this conversation makes us laugh in your face.

BRYCE: Hi, I'm Bryce Shivers.

LISA: And I'm Lisa Eversman. Do you ever cook something great and think: What could I possibly do to make this perfect dish *slightly* more perfect?

BRYCE: Shh! Lean in toward this book. We're about to whisper a secret ingredient that will improve **ANY** recipe you make.

BRYCE AND LISA: LAY AN EGG ON IT!

BRYCE: Is it laying or lying? Lie an egg? Lay?

LISA: Just *place* a fried egg on it.

BRYCE: Draping a fried egg atop your food will make *anything* taste better.

LISA: Well, maybe not anything, Bryce . . . Like . . . Not an omelet probably.

BRYCE: But otherwise: Anything!

LISA: There are a lot of other things that would be not-great with an egg on it.

BRYCE: No way! Come on! Like what, Lisa?

LISA: Most things. Name the first food that comes to mind.

BRYCE: An egg.

LISA: What else?

BRYCE: Toast!

LISA: I'm thinking about it, and maybe we should make a guide of some kind about where eggs can go. Maybe just look for this icon throughout the book, everyone: → That means: "This dish goes *great* with an egg on it."

BRYCE: Just make sure you fry 'em first! And CAREFUL: Frying pans are known to burn your hand.

BRYCE AND LISA: Here's the trick!

1. Take an Egg.
2. Put It on It.

01

SMALL PLATES

Sharing appetizers or small plates--at a tapas restaurant, for instance--can sometimes be a stressful experience. You have to negotiate "being polite" with the animal instinct to hiss opponents away from your share of the food. And ordering can be stressful, too . . . especially with a big group. You don't want to push your own ordering agenda too hard, but sometimes you really just want one thing. If it were up to you, the plan would be to order fifteen tiny plates of the tiny meatballs. But there are vegetarians to consider . . . and, generally, no one is really voicing what they want. So the group orders one of everything. And, inevitably, you end up in the tapas ghetto with a deviled egg someone split in half.

We have a trick for surviving small-plate dinners with large groups. The trick is: eat a small meal ahead of time. Don't expect to eat anything at the dinner party. But *do* expect to pay. And make sure to bring cash so you can get out of there quickly. And not just twenties--bring small bills.

—FRED AND CARRIE

THANKS!

Event Conversation

Dear Best Friends a Girl Could Ask For,
I want to thank each and every one of you for joining me in celebration of my 32nd (eek! ☺) birthday.

There is nothing that Lance and I would have liked to do more than have almost everyone I know sitting together at a huge table. And even though Lance wasn't there, Lance would have LOVED to be there. . . . As it turns out, he had an even bigger surprise planned for me the whole time, so not showing up was kind of a little trick that was part of the EVEN BIGGER surprise. (You wouldn't believe what he did, it was so romantic.)

Anyway, just a little Thank-You Note to say that I hope you enjoyed the VIP room at the restaurant. I also hope you loved all of the tapas, which were hand-picked from the menu by me. I just thought tapas would be a good idea because it would be fun to just have cute little plates, and everyone could try a little bite of something and trade plates with the person next to them and try a little bite of something else and then pass the plate or trade for a little bite of some other yummy little thing. I think we can all agree that the top tapas were:

* the bread and mushroom one
* those little cheesy meat-filled dates
* pork peppers
* What was that *tortilla* (Spanish omelet) with the little chips? What was that called?? SO YUMMY.

I asked the restaurant for the recipes so we can make them at home!

Anyway, only 357 days until my next birthday party. Who knows what the theme next year will be?! It's too early to start planning, he-he. But please make sure you save the date.

With our deepest Love and Gratitude,
Nina and Lance

Add a Comment

 Add a Photo

Nina
and
Lance

TAPAS BIRTHDAY PARTY

WILD MUSHROOM AND ARTICHOKE TARTINES

TOTAL: 40 MINUTES ★ SERVES 6

Lay an EGG on it!

1 lemon, halved, plus 2 tablespoons freshly squeezed lemon juice

1½ pounds baby artichokes

2 tablespoons extra-virgin olive oil

16 ounces mixed wild mushrooms, such as shiitake, cremini, oyster, or chanterelles, stemmed and thinly sliced (about 6 cups)

1 large shallot, finely chopped (about ¼ cup)

Kosher salt and freshly ground black pepper

2 tablespoons cognac

½ cup dry white wine, such as Albariño or Vinho Verde

½ cup low-sodium chicken broth

1 tablespoon chopped fresh savory or thyme

2 tablespoons unsalted butter

6 slices multigrain bread, toasted

1 garlic clove

1 Fill a bowl with water, squeeze the halved lemon into it, and then add the lemon halves. Pluck off the outer leaves of the artichokes, revealing a yellow-green core. Using a serrated knife, trim off the top third. Cut the artichokes into thin wedges and add them to the lemon water to prevent oxidizing.

2 In a large skillet, heat the oil until shimmering. Add the mushrooms and shallots. Season with salt and pepper to taste and cook over high heat, stirring once or twice, until browned, about 7 minutes.

3 Drain the artichokes, shaking off the excess water, and add them to the skillet. Stir and cook for 2 minutes.

4 Add the cognac and cook until evaporated.

5 Add the wine, broth, lemon juice, and savory, and season lightly with salt and pepper. Cover and simmer over medium heat until the artichokes are tender, about 5 minutes.

6 Remove the lid and cook until the liquid is nearly evaporated, 5 to 6 minutes. Stir in the butter.

7 Rub the toast on one side with the garlic clove and set on a platter. Spoon the vegetable mixture on top and serve right away.

Make ahead: The mushroom and artichoke mixture can be refrigerated overnight. Rewarm, adding a few tablespoons of water to loosen the mixture.

SAUTÉED SHRIMP WITH PIQUILLOS, OLIVES, AND PORK BELLY

ACTIVE: 30 MINUTES ★ TOTAL: 40 MINUTES ★ SERVES 4 TO 6

Kosher salt

4-ounce slice of pork belly, about ½ inch thick

3 tablespoons extra-virgin olive oil

12 ounces medium shrimp, shelled and deveined

2 large garlic cloves, thinly sliced

½ teaspoon smoked Spanish paprika

¼ cup sliced piquillo peppers

¼ cup coarsely chopped green Spanish olives

¼ cup dry white wine, such as Albariño

Crusty bread, for serving

1 Bring a medium saucepan of salted water to a boil. Add the pork belly and boil for 3 minutes. Drain, pat dry, and let cool.

2 Slice the pork belly into ¼-inch pieces.

3 In a large skillet, heat the oil. Add the pork belly and cook over medium-high heat, stirring occasionally, until crisp all over, about 5 minutes. Be careful about spattering oil. Using a slotted spoon, transfer the pork to a plate.

4 Add the shrimp, garlic, and paprika. Season with salt and cook over medium-high heat, stirring frequently, until the shrimp are just pink, about 1½ minutes. Add the peppers, olives, and wine and simmer until the liquid is reduced by half, about 1 minute. Add the pork and simmer for 1 minute. Serve right away with plenty of crusty bread.

BAKED MANCHEGO-FILLED DATES

TOTAL: 20 MINUTES ★ MAKES 48 PIECES

24 Medjool dates

⅓ cup (about 2 ounces) finely chopped serrano ham

½ cup shredded Manchego cheese (about 3 ounces)

24 Marcona almonds

1 Preheat the oven to 350°F. Make a small slash into each date and remove the pits, keeping them as intact as possible. Fill the cavities with ham, cheese, and almonds. Close slightly and transfer to a baking sheet.

2 Bake until warm and the cheese is melted, 8 to 10 minutes.

3 Transfer the dates to a platter and serve warm.

Make ahead: The dates can be stuffed and refrigerated overnight.

TORTILLA ESPAÑOLA

TOTAL: 20 MINUTES ★ SERVES 6

12 large eggs

1 5-ounce bag of flavored potato chips, lightly crushed (Black Pepper & Sea Salt; Crab; Bacon; Crawfish; Thai, etc.)

2 tablespoons extra-virgin olive oil

3 large scallions, sliced

3 ounces Spanish chorizo, finely chopped

Bread, for serving

1 Preheat the broiler and position a rack 8 inches from the heat.

2 In a large bowl, beat the eggs. Add the potato chips and let soak for 10 minutes.

3 In a large ovenproof nonstick skillet, heat the oil until shimmering. Add the scallions and chorizo and cook over high heat, stirring, until the chorizo has rendered its fat, about 2 to 3 minutes.

4 Add the potato chip–egg mixture, stirring to combine with the chorizo mixture. Cook over medium-high heat until the bottom and sides are set, about 3 minutes.

5 Broil the *tortilla* until the top is lightly browned and the eggs are set, 3 to 4 minutes longer. Slide the *tortilla* onto a plate, cut into wedges, and serve hot, warm, or at room temperature.

GARMIN'S CRISPY PORK RIBLETS

ACTIVE: 30 MINUTES ★ TOTAL: 3 HOURS PLUS
OVERNIGHT COOLING ★ SERVES 4 FOR MAIN
COURSE OR 8 AS AN APPETIZER

RIBS

2 medium racks (about 3 pounds) of spareribs,
   split lengthwise in half (see Note)

6 large garlic cloves, smashed

1 large onion, quartered

1 serrano chile or jalapeño, halved

4 lemongrass stalks, lightly smashed

8 ¼-inch slices fresh, peeled ginger

2 cups low-sodium chicken broth

½ cup soy sauce

½ cup cornstarch

½ cup all-purpose flour

Vegetable oil, for frying

Note: Have your butcher cut the racks lengthwise
into riblets for you.

GLAZE

¼ cup orange marmalade

¼ cup low-sodium chicken broth (or braising
   liquid from the ribs)

2 tablespoons ketchup

2 tablespoons mustard

1 tablespoon sesame oil

1 tablespoon Asian fish sauce

2 tablespoons Korean chili flakes (or Aleppo
   pepper flakes or 1 tablespoon crushed
   red pepper flakes)

2 tablespoons kosher salt

Garmin
- - - - - - - - - -

I'M A LITTLE GUY

Hey. My name is Garmin. I'm a little
guy. My fingers are small, my teeth are
little, and my metabolism is super-fast.
I eat small meals all throughout the day,
and I eat them quickly! Then I talk a lot
about what I ate. I can talk really fast
because it takes less energy to use my
voice. I'm a little guy!

1 Make the ribs: Preheat the oven to 350°F. Place the ribs into a large, heavy Dutch oven and add the garlic, onion, chile, lemongrass, ginger, broth, soy sauce, and 4 cups of water. Bring to a boil, uncovered.

2 Cover and braise in the oven until the ribs are tender, but not falling off the bone, about 2 hours. Occasionally turn the riblets in the liquid.

3 Transfer the riblets to a platter, pat dry, and refrigerate until very cold, about 4 hours, preferably overnight. Strain the cooking liquid, pour off the fat, and reserve for another use.

4 Cut the cold riblets between the bones and transfer to a large paper bag. In a small bowl, whisk the cornstarch and flour and add it to the ribs. Close the bag and shake until the riblets are coated. Turn the riblets out onto another paper bag and tap off the excess flour.

5 In a large saucepan, heat 2 inches of oil to 375°F. Working in 3 or 4 batches, fry the riblets, trying to maintain the heat at 360°F, until browned and crusty, about 6 minutes per batch. Drain on paper and continue with the remaining ribs.

6 Meanwhile, make the glaze: In a blender or mini food processor, puree the marmalade, broth, ketchup, mustard, sesame oil, and fish sauce and transfer to a small saucepan. Simmer over medium heat until glossy, about 5 minutes. In a small bowl, combine the Korean chile flakes and salt.

7 Transfer the riblets to a large bowl and toss with two-thirds of the sauce. Arrange on a platter and sprinkle with the chile-salt mixture. Serve with the remaining sauce on the side.

Make ahead: The riblets (un-fried) and glaze can be refrigerated separately for up to 5 days.

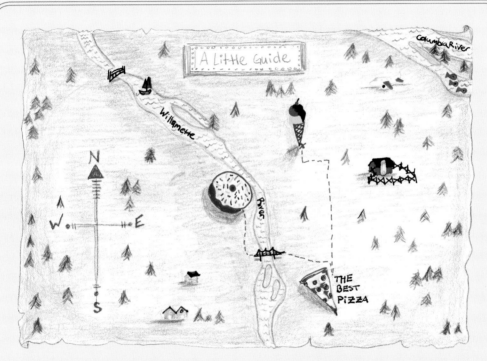

Garmin again! You might remember me from the other page over there. But maybe not, because I'm a little guy. I can dart around and slip in and out of places without people noticing me sometimes. I had some leftover energy, so I made this little guide to my favorite things to eat in Portland. If you don't feel like cooking at home, these are the best places to go. I know where the best places are because I've been all over the city with my scavenger hunt team. And when I do that much running around I get very hungry, so I keep eating and eating and eating. I've tried the food at practically every single place.

PRETZEL KNOTS

a favorite snack of the **PORTLAND KNOT STORE**

Sailor's Pretzel

Sea Salt 'N' Bread Rope

Hansel & Pretzel

Gentleman's Beer Dunker

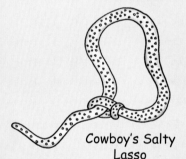
Cowboy's Salty Lasso

Wavy Bread

Widow's Up-Do

Knot Knot, Who's there? A Pretzel

Tiller's Kitchen Idea

The Bread Handshake

The Dark & Knotty

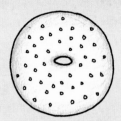

Nice Try, Bagel

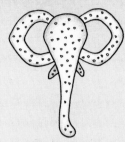

Day at the Zoo

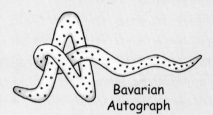

Bavarian Autograph

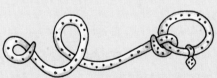

Gunner's Tie-Pretzel

The New York Bread Knot

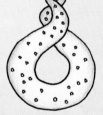

The Little Pretzel That Wanted to Be a Doughnut

Tie the Dog Up

Sourdough's Lark

Midshipman's Supper

The Pretzel of the United States of America

The Worm

Welcome to Around the World in 80 Plates.

Hello, I'm Johnny. As the first stop on your journey across the seven seas of flavor, I am pleased to present our World-Famous Sides 'n' Stuff! appetizer menu. As you wander across this Map of Apps you will uncover that each app is a fun fusion of your favorite finger foods. And good news, explorers: *all* these apps (minus the cheese boats) can be served on a skewer, stacked in a pyramid, in a souvenir globe, in a waffle fry basket, or even wrapped in a lettuce cup if you're looking to lighten your load. Cheese boats can only be served in baked potatoes.

>> **Crispy Cheese**

>> **Duck Triangles**

>> **Buffalo Bombers**

>> **Cheese Boats**

>> **Potato Tornados**

>> **Chicken Crusters**

>> **Beef Dingers**

>> **Deep-Fried Salad**

>> **Crusty Chicken Crusters**

>> **The Rachel**

>> **Quadruple Dippers**

>> **Zing the Blues**

>> **The Perfect Egg Roll**

>> **Cheesy Beefees**

* SIDES 'N' STUFF ARE ALSO AVAILABLE
  ON A BORING, TYPICAL PLATE.

CHEESY BEEFEES

ACTIVE: 20 MINUTES ★ TOTAL: 45 MINUTES ★
SERVES 6 TO 8

2 slices good-quality packaged white bread,
shredded

2 tablespoons half-and-half or milk

1 large egg

2 scallions, minced

2 garlic cloves, minced

1 large jalapeño, seeded and minced

2 tablespoons chopped fresh cilantro

1½ teaspoons kosher salt

¾ pound ground sirloin

¾ pound ground chuck

Vegetable oil, for brushing the pan

2 ounces pepper jack cheese, cut into
24 ½-inch cubes

¼ cup plus 2 tablespoons freshly
grated Parmigiano-Reggiano

1 Preheat the oven to 425°F and
position a rack on the upper
shelf.

2 In a large bowl, combine the
bread, half-and-half, and egg and
squeeze to a paste.

3 Add the scallions, garlic, jalapeño,
cilantro, and salt and stir to
combine.

4 Add the sirloin and chuck and work
with your hands until evenly combined.

5 Brush a nonstick baking sheet with oil.
Form the meat into 24 balls, using lightly
moistened hands. Tuck a cube of the pepper
jack cheese into each meatball and seal.
Arrange the meatballs on the baking sheet
and roast until firm and lightly browned,
about 12 minutes.

6 Remove the baking sheet from the oven
and turn the oven up to Broil.

7 Transfer the meatballs to a large bowl
and toss with ¼ cup of the grated
Parmigiano-Romano. Return the meatballs to
the baking sheet, spacing them very closely
together, and sprinkle with the remaining 2
tablespoons of the grated cheese.

8 Broil on the top rack, watching carefully
until browned and sizzling, 2 to 3
minutes longer, shifting the pan for even
browning. Transfer to a platter and serve with
toothpicks and napkins.

AROUND THE
WORLD
— IN —
80 PLATES

BRUSSELS SPROUTS WITH BACON

TOTAL: 30 MINUTES ★ SERVES 6

Lay an EGG on it!

½ cup hazelnuts

1 pound medium-size Brussels sprouts (walnut size), trimmed and halved

3 tablespoons extra-virgin olive oil

Kosher salt and freshly ground black pepper

4 ounces thick-cut bacon, cut into ½-inch pieces

1 large shallot, very thinly sliced (about ½ cup)

2 tablespoons sherry vinegar

1 Preheat the oven to 350°F. Spread the hazelnuts on a pie plate and toast until fragrant and the skins blister, about 12 minutes. Let cool, then rub the hazelnuts together in a clean kitchen towel to remove the skins. Coarsely chop the nuts.

2 In a bowl, toss the Brussels sprouts with the oil and season with salt and pepper to taste. Heat a large skillet until very hot. Add the Brussels sprouts, cut side down, and cook over high heat until browned, about 5 minutes. Flip the Brussels sprouts, cover, and cook until crisp-tender, about 3 minutes longer. Transfer to a plate.

3 Add the bacon to the pan and cook over medium heat until crisp and browned, about 5 minutes.

4 Add the shallots and cook, stirring, until softened and lightly browned, about 5 minutes.

5 Add the Brussels sprouts and toss to combine. Add the vinegar and cook until the vinegar is nearly evaporated.

6 Stir in the hazelnuts and serve right away.

FOOD PHOTOGRAPHY

When photographing chefs for magazines or dining guides, make sure to have them hold the food in an unnatural way that seems awkward and rock-and-roll-y. Play hip-hop music really loud. Make sure to get them to spill things. Dump things. Like they don't even need the ingredients anymore. Flour makes really good clouds. They should maybe hop up on the stove. We recommend these Brussels sprouts because they are easy to indifferently throw at the camera.

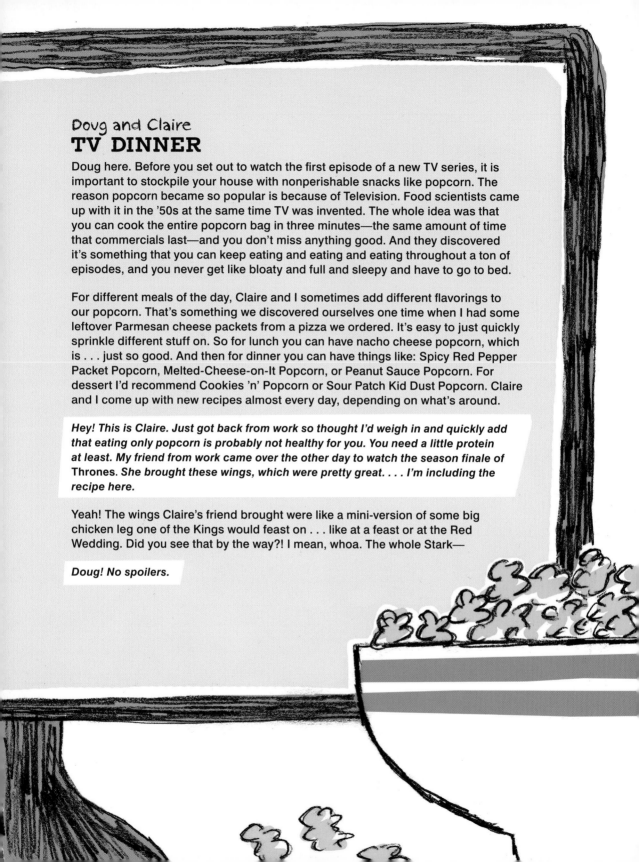

Doug and Claire
TV DINNER

Doug here. Before you set out to watch the first episode of a new TV series, it is important to stockpile your house with nonperishable snacks like popcorn. The reason popcorn became so popular is because of Television. Food scientists came up with it in the '50s at the same time TV was invented. The whole idea was that you can cook the entire popcorn bag in three minutes—the same amount of time that commercials last—and you don't miss anything good. And they discovered it's something that you can keep eating and eating and eating throughout a ton of episodes, and you never get like bloaty and full and sleepy and have to go to bed.

For different meals of the day, Claire and I sometimes add different flavorings to our popcorn. That's something we discovered ourselves one time when I had some leftover Parmesan cheese packets from a pizza we ordered. It's easy to just quickly sprinkle different stuff on. So for lunch you can have nacho cheese popcorn, which is . . . just so good. And then for dinner you can have things like: Spicy Red Pepper Packet Popcorn, Melted-Cheese-on-It Popcorn, or Peanut Sauce Popcorn. For dessert I'd recommend Cookies 'n' Popcorn or Sour Patch Kid Dust Popcorn. Claire and I come up with new recipes almost every day, depending on what's around.

Hey! This is Claire. Just got back from work so thought I'd weigh in and quickly add that eating only popcorn is probably not healthy for you. You need a little protein at least. My friend from work came over the other day to watch the season finale of Thrones. *She brought these wings, which were pretty great. . . . I'm including the recipe here.*

Yeah! The wings Claire's friend brought were like a mini-version of some big chicken leg one of the Kings would feast on . . . like at a feast or at the Red Wedding. Did you see that by the way?! I mean, whoa. The whole Stark—

Doug! No spoilers.

NACHO CHEESE POPCORN

TOTAL: 20 MINUTES ★ SERVES 6

¼ cup cheddar cheese powder or 1 packet
    cheese powder from packaged mac
    and cheese
1 tablespoon nutritional yeast
1 teaspoon onion powder
Scant ¼ teaspoon chipotle powder
¼ cup plus 2 tablespoons vegetable oil
⅔ cup popping corn
4 tablespoons unsalted butter, melted
Kosher salt

1 In a small bowl, combine the cheddar
powder, nutritional yeast, onion powder,
and chipotle powder.

2 In a large pot, heat the oil. Add the
popping corn, cover (leaving the lid
slightly ajar to allow steam to vent), and pop
over medium heat, shaking the pan until
the popping slows to 2-second intervals.
Immediately turn the popped corn out into a
large bowl and drizzle with the butter.

3 Add half the seasoning mixture and toss.
Add the remaining mixture and toss
again. Season with salt if desired.

Make ahead: The seasoning mixture can
be refrigerated for up to 2 months.

CLAIRE'S CO-WORKER'S SICHUAN CHICKEN WINGS

ACTIVE: 20 MINUTES ★ TOTAL 1¼ HOURS ★ SERVES 4 TO 6

WINGS

2 tablespoons ground cumin

1½ teaspoons crushed red pepper flakes

½ teaspoon Chinese 5-spice powder

2 teaspoons kosher salt

¼ cup all-purpose flour

8 large chicken wings (about 3 pounds), split into wingettes and drumettes

1½ tablespoons canola oil, plus more for brushing

Sliced scallions, for garnish

Fresh cilantro leaves, for garnish

DUCK-LIKE SAUCE

2 tablespoons soy sauce

½ cup apricot preserves

1½ teaspoons minced fresh, peeled ginger

1 Preheat the oven to 425°F and line a large rimmed baking sheet with parchment paper.

2 In a large bowl, combine the cumin, red pepper flakes, 5-spice powder, salt, and flour.

3 On a work surface, coat the chicken with the 1½ tablespoons of oil, rubbing to coat completely. Add the chicken to the spice-and-flour blend and toss to coat completely. Arrange the chicken on the baking sheet and brush lightly with oil.

4 Roast in the center of the oven until deeply browned and crispy, turning once or twice, about 50 minutes. Blot on paper towels to remove the excess fat.

5 Meanwhile, make the Duck-Like Sauce: In a food processor, combine the soy sauce, apricot preserves, and ginger with ¼ cup of water and puree until smooth. Transfer to a small saucepan and simmer on low heat until reduced to about ½ cup, 5 to 6 minutes. Pour the sauce into a small dipping bowl.

6 Arrange the wings on a platter, garnish with the scallions and cilantro, and serve with the sauce.

Make ahead: The sauce can be refrigerated for up to 1 month.

CINETOPIA

ARTISANAL MOVIE THEATER

Dear Movie Theater Workers,

As you know we are implementing a new Artisanal Menu at our theatrical concession stands at this theater and at our Beaverton location. We're just trying it out and hoping it goes well at these two locations before implementing this menu at our other two locations. Not certain it will stick forever, but just giving it a shot. We'll see how this goes.

Please adhere to the following substitutions and instructions to enhance the artisan concession aspect of the moviegoing experience. There will be supplies in the cupboards. Please follow instructions carefully, and don't forget to remind people about what we're doing here.

Note: Understanding that we've always been attentive to cleanliness, we actually want to keep it kind of messy now that we're going Artisan. Not, like, gross messy. Just borderline sloppy to remind people that it's handmade.

POPCORN

★ No longer use those white-and-red boxes. Instead, roll up a cone of newspaper. (We are using *Bridgetown Weekly* because they're free and they always drop off a ton of them in the lobby.)

★ Ask people (with kind of a wary tone) if they want butter. If so, tell them we temporarily do not have butter because we are working on sourcing it from a qualified local dairy farm. But then reassure them that, as flavoring, we have a new line of artisanal salts from that Salt Store on Mississippi, including: **Sea Salt** and **Truffle Salt.**

Note: If they go for truffle salt, please just put a little on there because it is expensive. Actually, don't even offer truffle salt to every single person. Just the people who seem unhappy about the no-butter thing.

SODA

★ We now only have Coca-Cola, and it is the authentic glass-bottle kind!

★ Patrons may not bring glass into the theater. It's always been the policy, and unfortunately we can't change it. So someone should stand by the theater door and request that patrons finish their glass-bottle Coca-Colas before entering.

CANDY

★ Candy-wise, we will be selling pretty much the same old stuff. Just please take all wrapping off of candy bars, licorice, etc., before serving. You can just hand it to them. Apparently that's what candymen used to do at old-tyme sweet shoppes.

★ ★ ★

AS A REMINDER, MOVING FORWARD, REFER TO THE "THEATER" AS "THE CINEMA" AND MOVIES AS "FILMS."

GRILLED FRUIT SUMMER ROLLS WITH PASSION FRUIT DIPPING SAUCE

TOTAL: 40 MINUTES ★ MAKES 8 SUMMER ROLLS

DIPPING SAUCE

½ cup passion fruit puree or juice

2 tablespoons freshly squeezed orange juice

3 tablespoons sugar (or more to taste)

½ teaspoon cornstarch dissolved in
    1 tablespoon water

1 tablespoon chopped fresh mint

ROLLS

1 large ripe mango, halved, peeled, and cut
    lengthwise into ⅓-inch-thick slices

¼ large ripe pineapple, peeled, cored, and
    cut into 8 (4 × ½-inch) spears

1 large, firm but ripe banana, peeled and halved
    lengthwise

Sugar, for sprinkling the fruit

2 ¾-inch-thick slices of pound cake (about
    6 ounces)

1 tablespoon unsalted butter, softened

8 large (7- to 8-inch) round rice paper wrappers

16 large fresh mint leaves

Chopped peanuts, for garnish

1 In a small saucepan, combine the passion fruit with the orange juice, the 3 tablespoons of sugar, and the cornstarch dissolved in the water. Whisk until smooth. Bring to a boil, then simmer until slightly thickened, about 30 seconds. Transfer to a bowl and refrigerate until chilled or overnight. Stir in the chopped mint.

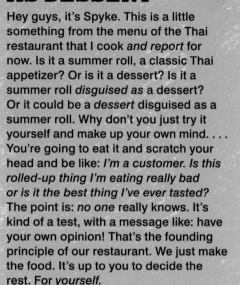

APPETIZER DISGUISED AS DESSERT

Hey guys, it's Spyke. This is a little something from the menu of the Thai restaurant that I cook *and report* for now. Is it a summer roll, a classic Thai appetizer? Or is it a dessert? Is it a summer roll *disguised as* a dessert? Or it could be a *dessert* disguised as a summer roll. Why don't you just try it yourself and make up your own mind. . . . You're going to eat it and scratch your head and be like: *I'm a customer. Is this rolled-up thing I'm eating really bad or is it the best thing I've ever tasted?* The point is: *no one* really knows. It's kind of a test, with a message like: have your own opinion! That's the founding principle of our restaurant. We just make the food. It's up to you to decide the rest. For *yourself.*

2 Preheat a grill pan and lightly oil the grates. Sprinkle the mango, pineapple, and banana with sugar. Spread the pound cake with the butter and set aside.

3 Grill the fruit over high heat, turning once, until lightly charred, about 1 minute for the bananas and 3 to 4 minutes for the mango and pineapple. Transfer to a plate and let cool.

4 Grill the pound cake until toasted on both sides, about 4 minutes.

5 Cut each banana half in half crosswise and half again lengthwise so you have 8 spears. Cut the pound cake into ¾-inch sticks.

6 Fill a skillet with warm water. Working with 1 rice paper wrapper at a time, dip the wrapper into the warm water, then transfer it to a work surface and blot it dry with paper towels. Let it sit for about 30 seconds to 1 minute until pliable. Arrange 2 mint leaves on the lower third of the wrapper and top with a piece of pineapple, mango, banana, and pound cake. Roll up into a tight cylinder, tucking in the sides as you roll up. Repeat with the remaining wrappers and filling.

7 Cut each roll in half and arrange on a platter. Sprinkle with the chopped peanuts and serve with the dipping sauce.

Make ahead: You can make the dipping sauce the day before you make the summer rolls.

A MESSAGE FROM THE MAYOR
— THE PRIDE OF —
PORTLAND

Citizens of Portland, put on your bibs! Our city's 3-D printer is officially plugged in and ready to feed our hungry. We are still in an early stage of figuring out how it works, but the manual indicates that dinner-for-all is in our city's not-too-distant future. The pride of Portland (our printer!) is sure to enhance our national reputation as a food destination. And as a Green City! Just think: edible forks and knives, freshly printed and ready to use for eating (and *to eat* after using!). This is a new vision of sustainability for our fair city: "All taste, no waste." I have searched and browsed the possibilities on an array of inspiring websites. There are all kinds of ideas out there (some *unbelievably* artistic!). Friends, it would be possible to print out a pizza *shaped like the state of Oregon!* With toppings that accurately reflect our great state's geography. Think of what our local culinary community could create with the right ingredient cartridges. The other night, I awoke to my own vision of a turkey jerky bass strap. Citizens, lend me your recipes! Let us dine together at the communal table *that is Portland, Oregon!*

We can pickle THAT!

EVERYTHING
SHOULD
BE PICKLED

We can pickle THAT!

BRYCE: Okay, so what you do is you take something and pickle it.

LISA: First you make the brine.

BRYCE: No one knows this, but pickling brine is delicious on its own. Just as a drink! Here, try it!

LISA: I'd rather just eat something pickled, thanks. Anything other than just straight brine.

BRYCE: They call it a "pickleback"!

LISA: Instead let's pickle . . . hmm, what do we have around here . . . an egg?

BRYCE: Pickled eggs. You just, wow . . . you described—like, actually my dream food. Anyway, see you tomorrow. I'm going to go take a sleeping pill and try really hard to dream about eating a pickled egg.

LISA: Or we could just pickle this egg.

BRYCE: Let's pickle that. Right away.

LISA: It's pickled.

BRYCE: And there are so many other things out there you can go ahead and pickle at home!

LISA: Carrots! Okra! Beets! Broccoli!

BRYCE: Shoes!

LISA: You're going to be great at pickling. You've got this! You can pickle this! We know you can pickle this . . .

BRYCE: Just pick something and go ahead and pickle it. We're rooting for you.

BRYCE AND LISA: Pickle it!

SPICY GARLIC PICKLES

ACTIVE: 20 MINUTES ★ TOTAL: 20 MINUTES
PLUS OVERNIGHT ★ MAKES 2 QUARTS

1½ pounds Kirby cucumbers, ends scrubbed

3 tablespoons kosher salt

2 tablespoons sugar

1¼ cups distilled white vinegar (5% acidity)

2 tablespoons whole coriander seeds

1 teaspoon whole black peppercorns

1 teaspoon allspice berries

2 cups water, plus more if necessary

4 to 6 long red or green hot chiles, halved lengthwise

6 large garlic cloves, halved

1 Pack the cucumbers into 2 quart-size jars.

2 In another quart-size jar, combine the salt, sugar, vinegar, coriander seeds, peppercorns, and allspice berries.

3 Close the lid and shake until the salt and sugar are dissolved.

4 Add the 2 cups of water and pour the brine over the pickles.

5 Tuck the chiles and garlic between the cucumbers.

6 Add enough water just to cover the pickles and keep them submerged. Cover and refrigerate overnight.

7 Can be stored in fridge for up to 2 months.

··· CUCUMBERS ···

12 ounces Kirby or Persian minis per quart-size jar. Wash and dry well, then trim the ends and pack into the jar.

··· CARROTS ···

12 ounces baby carrots per quart-size jar. Scrub, then blanch in boiling water for 2 minutes. Drain and cool under running water. Pack into the jar.

··· OKRA ···

12 ounces per quart-size jar. Wash and dry well and trim the stem end slightly, leaving the cap on. Pack into the jar.

··· ONIONS AND BEETS ···

6 ounces each cooked baby beets and peeled pearl onions per quart-size jar. Pack into the jar.

··· BROCCOLI STEMS ···

12 ounces per quart-size jar. Peel stems and cut into sticks. Pack into the jar.

BORSCHT WITH PICKLES, EGGS, AND HORSERADISH CREAM

TOTAL: 15 MINUTES ★ SERVES 4

1 tablespoon vegetable oil

1 small onion, minced (about ¼ cup)

1 cup coarsely shredded beets (suggest using a julienne peeler)

1 cup coarsely shredded carrots

Kosher salt and freshly ground black pepper

2 tablespoons red wine vinegar

1½ cups fresh beet juice (if using freshly juiced beets, scoop off any foam)

2 large eggs

4 fingerling potatoes

1 tablespoon prepared horseradish

¼ cup sour cream

8 cornichons, thinly sliced, for garnish

Dill sprigs, for garnish

1 In a medium saucepan, heat the oil. Cook the onion over medium heat, stirring, until softened, about 3 minutes. Add the beets and cook, stirring frequently, until just softened, about 3 minutes. Add the carrots, season with salt and pepper to taste, and cook until just softened, 3 minutes. Add the vinegar and cook until evaporated.

2 Add the beet juice and transfer to a medium bowl. Refrigerate the borscht until chilled.

Marco
- - - - - - - - -

911 BEETS

Marco here. If you have an emergency, dial 911. If you're eating beets and you *think* you are dealing with an emergency, we have a new number we would ask you to call. Ready?

For beets: 111

Please pay special attention to borscht, the most regularly reported case of beet-related trauma. Always remember: "Borscht IS Beets." We encourage you to remember this via the following acronym: B.I.B.

Now take a deep breath and calmly enjoy your borscht.

Thank you.

3 In a small saucepan, cover the eggs with cold water and bring to a vigorous boil. Cover and let sit off the heat for 12 minutes. Drain and shake the pan to crack the eggs lightly. Add ice water to cool. Peel and chop the eggs.

4 Meanwhile, fill the saucepan with water and bring to a boil. Add the potatoes and boil until they are tender, about 10 minutes. Drain, cool completely, and cut into coins.

5 In a small bowl, combine the horseradish and sour cream. Serve the borscht in small bowls and garnish with the horseradish cream, chopped eggs, potatoes, cornichons, and dill.

Dear Brendan and Michelle,

On behalf of the collective of farmers and families whose labors and love have resulted in this hand-delivered cardboard box of beautiful produce, we would like to say: greetings! And thank you for skipping the grocery store and supporting local Portland agriculture by ordering these vegetables directly to your home.

Allow us to walk you through the contents of this box so you know what you're dealing with here . . . and where it comes from (. . . *here!*). As usual, we are enclosing our weekly recipe suggestions! But feel free to use this beautiful produce however you see fit. The recipe suggestions are just a fun thing we do now. How you feel like preparing these beautiful vegetables is up to you. (Not us!) ;)

The beautiful corn contained in this box comes from Harvey Baker's farm. Harvey wanted to let you all know that you're all welcome to swing by his farm. Just let Harvey know first. Call him like a day ahead of time, please. No big groups. And keep your voice down around the gray horse if you decide to come by. Thank you, and enjoy the fresh corn!

It's turnip time! Turnip the volume, everybody. Time to celebrate the turnip with a celebratory snack. These beautiful turnips are from Lane Potter's turnip patch. She is the proud keeper of Oregon's only turnip patch, Potter's Turnip Patch, dedicated strictly to turnips. It's the only turnip-only patch in Oregon, so she knows what she's doing here, guys. You'll agree when you taste the turnips from this patch of hers. Enjoy your turnips!

The carrots are the prize item in this week's CSA box. (Shh! Don't tell the corn, turnip, or beet guys.) But it's true. Carrots have never been crunchier or as naturally orange. The dirt on them is intentionally left there by the farmers. It's not that they are lazy or that the farms are too understaffed to have appointed carrot-cleaners. We have guys who could theoretically do that. No, we left the dirt there because it is a nice way of reminding you that these beautiful carrots were dug up from the ground by some local guys who affectionately placed them in this box. If you have kids at home, it is nice to show them the dirt on the carrots so they learn that carrots come from the ground, not the grocery store.

Pay attention to the beets in this box. Do not forget that you ate them. If they're missing all of a sudden, ask yourself: Did I eat those beets at some point? You want to keep track. If you experience any unusual body-stuff, remind yourself: it might be beets. Then calmly think if you ate beets. Then remember that you did and safely go on with your day. *A message from 111, Portland's Local Beets Beat.*

Thank you for supporting Community Supported Agriculture, *Brendan and Michelle*! Have a beautiful week. And see you next week. It's supposed to be a sunny week.

Sincerely,
Your CSA Family and Friends

Brendan
and
Michelle

AUTUMN MARKET BASKET SALAD

ROASTED ROOT VEGETABLES AND GREENS WITH NUTTY RANCH DRESSING

ACTIVE: 30 MINUTES ★ TOTAL: 1½ HOURS ★
SERVES 6

½ cup walnut halves

8 baby beets (about 1½ to 2 inches), preferably
   golden or chioggia, scrubbed

8 baby turnips, trimmed

1 bunch fresh baby carrots, scrubbed

4 unpeeled garlic cloves

4 sprigs of fresh thyme

¼ cup water

¼ cup plus 2 tablespoons extra-virgin olive oil

Kosher salt and freshly ground black pepper

¼ cup mayonnaise

2 tablespoons whole or low-fat plain Greek
   yogurt or sour cream

1 tablespoon distilled white vinegar

¼ cup buttermilk

8 ounces mixed greens, such as mesclun,
   baby arugula, and watercress (thick
   stems discarded)

1 Preheat the oven to 350°F.

2 Spread the walnuts out on a pie plate and toast until golden and fragrant, about 10 minutes. Let cool. Finely chop the walnuts.

3 Meanwhile, in a large baking dish, arrange the beets in one third, the turnips in another third, and the carrots in the last third. Scatter the garlic and thyme all around and drizzle with the water and 2 tablespoons of the oil. Season with salt and pepper to taste.

4 Cover with foil and roast until tender, about 45 minutes. Remove the foil and roast until the liquid is mostly evaporated, about 10 minutes longer.

5 Let cool, then peel the beets and cut them into halves (quarters if large). Cut the turnips into halves (quarters if large) and the carrots in half (lengthwise if large.)

6 Squeeze the garlic cloves from their skins into a small bowl and mash to a paste. Whisk in the mayonnaise, yogurt, and vinegar until smooth. Whisk in the buttermilk, followed by the remaining ¼ cup of oil. Season with ½ teaspoon each salt and pepper. Fold in half of the walnuts.

7 In a bowl, toss the greens with the roasted vegetables and ⅓ cup of the dressing and arrange on a platter. Garnish with the remaining walnuts and serve the remaining dressing on the side.

SUMMER MARKET BASKET SALAD

TOMATOES AND SNAP PEAS WITH ROASTED CORN-CHILE DRESSING

ACTIVE: 30 MINUTES ★ TOTAL: 40 MINUTES ★ SERVES 6

1 large jalapeño

1 ear of corn, husked

¼ cup canola oil, plus more for brushing

2 tablespoons freshly squeezed lime juice

1 scallion, whites and greens, thinly sliced separately

2 tablespoons chopped fresh cilantro, plus leaves for garnish

Kosher salt

12 ounces mixed heirloom tomatoes, cut into slices, halves, and quarters for variety

2 ounces sugar snap peas, thinly sliced on the bias

1 Brush the jalapeño and corn lightly with oil and roast over a gas flame, turning frequently until browned all over, about 5 minutes. Let cool, then peel, seed, and chop the jalapeño and remove the kernels from the cob.

2 In a mini food processor, combine the lime juice with the ¼ cup of oil and process until combined. Add the jalapeño, scallion whites, and half of the corn and pulse to a chunky dressing. Add the chopped cilantro and pulse to combine. Season with salt to taste.

3 In a large bowl, toss the tomatoes, snap peas, scallion greens, and remaining roasted corn with some of the dressing and arrange on plates. Drizzle the remaining dressing on top and garnish with cilantro leaves. Serve right away.

02

MAIN COURSES

There are so many restaurants in Portland to choose from. You could eat at a different place every day of the year, and probably only a handful of the places you'd go to wouldn't be *that* great. Going out is fun, but there is also something really thrilling about cooking something restaurant worthy in your own kitchen at home. Especially on a rainy night . . . which is most nights in Portland.

When attempting the following main courses at home, pay attention to the presentation of the dish. That's a big part of restaurant experience here. Arrange the food carefully on the plate and maybe consider "propping it" where appropriate with things like radishes curled up into flower-shapes and little drips of colorful sauce. Dim the lights in your living room. Light some candles. Put the bread directly on the table without a basket or a plate for the "rustic" effect. Consider dusting the table with flour, just in the area where the bread goes. And maybe hire a string band to play in one of the corners of the room.

Finally, invite some strangers over to populate the other tables you've set up in your dining room. This way, there is no need to go out on a rainy night!

—FRED AND CARRIE

Claire

LOCAVORE DINNER PARTY

I took Doug with me to this dinner party the other day—it was a *locavore* dinner party, which basically means: all of the food was *extremely* local. Like, foraged from the land within five blocks of the house. One of the main courses was a fish that our host had caught from the Burnside Bridge with his Fishing Society right by the skate park. I didn't even know there were fish in the Willamette you could eat, but apparently it's a thing.

There was also a delicious mushroom dish. On the napkins was a hand-illustrated guide of poisonous versus nonpoisonous mushrooms growing in the neighborhood. It was really crafty and interesting.

It was a potluck dinner, so Doug and I were supposed to bring something locally foraged, too. We went on a walk around the block, mostly in people's backyards, looking for edible things. We found a plum tree at our neighbor's place, but we would have had to take a lot of them, which seemed sketchy. This guy down the street has a chicken coop . . . but that seemed really complicated even if we just tiptoed in there and took a couple of eggs. The chickens did not seem friendly.

We ended up bringing some mint from our backyard. I used it to make mint lemonade. And Doug made a mix tape to play at the party, which went over really well.

ROASTED WILD MUSHROOMS WITH FORAGED GREENS AND HAZELNUT VINAIGRETTE

ACTIVE: 30 MINUTES ★ TOTAL: 50 MINUTES ★ SERVES 4

1 pound mixed wild mushrooms, such as chanterelles, shiitake, matsutake, oyster, king oyster, shimeji, or lobster mushrooms, sliced, quartered, or whole if small

½ teaspoon chopped fresh thyme

½ teaspoon chopped fresh rosemary

2 tablespoons unsalted butter, melted

2 tablespoons plus 3 tablespoons extra-virgin olive oil

Kosher salt and freshly ground black pepper

½ cup hazelnuts

1 tablespoon plus 1 teaspoon hazelnut oil

4 large eggs

1 tablespoon red wine vinegar

1 small garlic clove, grated on a microplane

5 ounces mixed baby wild greens, such as baby kale, watercress, dandelion, arugula

2 ounces shaved hard cheese, such as Sardinian Pecorino, Manchego, dry Jack

1 Preheat the oven to 450°F. Line a large baking sheet with parchment paper.

2 In a bowl, combine the mushrooms, thyme, rosemary, butter, and 2 tablespoons of the oil and toss to coat. Spread on the baking sheet and roast until browned and tender, about 20 minutes, stirring once or twice. Season with salt and pepper to taste and let cool.

3 Spread the hazelnuts on a pie plate and toast until fragrant and the skins blister, about 8 minutes. Transfer the nuts to a kitchen towel and rub off the skins. Coarsely chop the nuts and toss with 1 teaspoon of the hazelnut oil. Season with salt to taste and set aside.

4 In a large bowl, whisk the vinegar with the garlic, the remaining 3 tablespoons of olive oil, and the remaining 1 tablespoon of hazelnut oil. Season with salt and pepper to taste.

5 Add the mushrooms, greens, cheese, and hazelnuts and toss to combine.

6 Prepare the eggs. Crack the eggs into individual ramekins, being careful not to break the yolks. Bring a deep skillet of water to a boil and season with salt. Reduce the heat to low and one by one pour each egg into the simmering water, leaving space between the eggs. Poach the eggs until the whites are set but the yolks are still runny, about 3 minutes. Using a slotted spoon, transfer the eggs to a paper towel–lined plate and gently pat dry.

7 To serve, transfer the salad to plates and top each with a poached egg.

Make ahead: The mushrooms and dressing can be refrigerated separately for up to 3 days.

CEDAR-PLANKED SALMON WITH TANGY RADISH SLAW

ACTIVE: 15 MINUTES ★ TOTAL: 2 HOURS,
35 MINUTES ★ SERVES 4

1 large cedar plank
1 teaspoon sugar
1 teaspoon ground cumin
1 teaspoon pure ancho chile powder
1 teaspoon kosher salt
1 teaspoon freshly ground pepper
2 pounds center-cut salmon fillet, such as
    Chinook (king) or sockeye, skin on, about
    1½ inches thick, pin bones removed
1 tablespoon extra-virgin olive oil, plus more
    for brushing
3 large radishes (about 5 ounces), cut into fine
    matchsticks (about 1 cup)
1 large scallion, thinly sliced
½ small Thai chile, minced (about ¼ teaspoon)
1 tablespoon chopped fresh flat-leaf parsley
1½ teaspoons freshly squeezed lemon juice

1 Soak the cedar plank in warm water for
2 hours.

2 In a small bowl, combine the sugar,
cumin, chile powder, salt, and pepper.
Brush the salmon all over with oil and rub
with the spice mixture. Let sit for 15 minutes.

3 In a bowl, toss the radishes with the
scallion, chile, parsley, lemon juice, and
1 tablespoon of olive oil. Season with salt
and pepper to taste.

4 Light a grill and drain the cedar plank.
Pat dry. Set the salmon on the plank,
skin side down, and place on the grill. Cover
and cook over high heat until the plank
begins to smoke and the salmon is cooked
through, about 20 minutes for king salmon
and about 10 minutes for sockeye, which is
thinner and less fatty. Serve the salmon with
the radish slaw.

Roasted Wild Mushrooms with Foraged Greens and Hazelnut Vinaigrette

Mint Lemonade

Cedar-Planked Salmon with Tangy Radish Slaw

KATH AND DAVE'S

GUIDE TO PICKING A TABLE AT A RESTAURANT

When you go to a restaurant, you have a right—as a *paying* customer—to move from table to table. Do not be afraid to constantly move around. Maybe you sit down and look at the menu at one table,[1] but then you notice that it is too close to a vent. Get up and change tables if the vent is:[2]

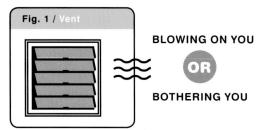

Fig. 1 / Vent

BLOWING ON YOU

OR

BOTHERING YOU

If you're eating your appetizers at a table by the door and a booth becomes available, move to the booth.[3] You can just carry your plates and silverware across the room. They don't mind the help! If the sun comes out from behind a building and starts blinding you, or they sat you right next to a speaker and it's thumping in your ear, just get up and move. We recommend facing the door, in general.[4] Just to keep an eye on who is coming in and out of the restaurant. We also suggest sitting with a view of the kitchen while they are making your food,[5] and then moving over to the window when it is time to eat.[6] (Just to get away from all the kitchen noise and smells and racket.)

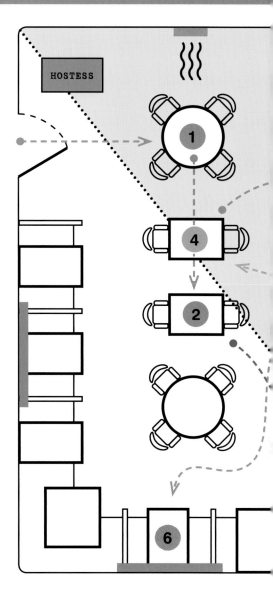

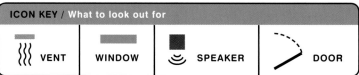

ICON KEY / What to look out for

| VENT | WINDOW | SPEAKER | DOOR |

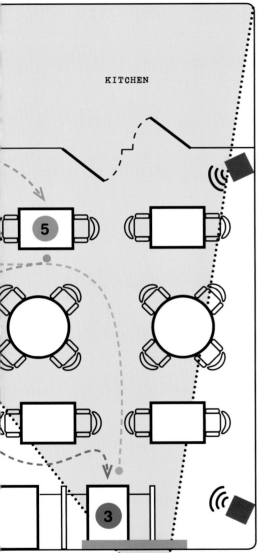

KITCHEN

5

3

HOT
ZONE

In case you are seated at an uneven, rocking table, we recommend bringing a wedge of wood with you to the restaurant. Just stick it under the leg of the table so it stops rocking around. Rolled-up newspaper or napkins just don't work as well. The restaurant will thank you.

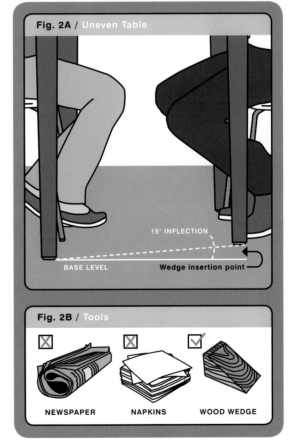

Fig. 2A / Uneven Table

15° INFLECTION

BASE LEVEL   Wedge insertion point

Fig. 2B / Tools

| NEWSPAPER | NAPKINS | WOOD WEDGE |

REMEMBER, THE WAITSTAFF DOES NOT MIND MOVING YOU.

Peter
and
Nance
- - - - - - - - - -

ORDERING
THE CHICKEN

Nance and I have been living together in Portland for—how long has it been? Maybe ten years? That can't—is it possible? Fifteen? Twenty? You and me?

Peter knows exactly how long it's been. Our anniversary is coming up soon so he's just teasing me. Very funny, mister.

Me? And *you*?

The city of Portland brought Peter and me together in the first place. And our love for each other is continually renewed by date nights and other adventures out in this town.

So I take her out on these dates . . . and the food here in Portland is just great. Let me tell you. The things you can eat! For dinner? Lunch? So many options and choices and things you can have or not have, depending on what you want . . .

And *local* and *sustainable*. You can eat *consciously* and *ethically*. That's something Peter and I also have in common. We care about our choices. And we would encourage you to do the same.

Not in a pushy way—just a friendly version of encouraging.

When ordering at a restaurant, ask questions. Find out if your food is *local* and, if so, *how* local? Was it ethically raised, and *by whom*?

Ask yourself: Who are these people?

Ask the questions you want answers to.

BUTTERFLIED CHICKEN ROASTED OVER BREAD

ACTIVE: 30 MINUTES ★ TOTAL: 1½ HOURS ★
SERVES 4 TO 6

1 pound small Italian or Japanese eggplants, cut into 1½-inch chunks

1 1-pound loaf of Italian bread, cut into 1½-inch chunks

½ cup pitted Sicilian green olives

1 tablespoon harissa or sambal

2 garlic cloves, minced

1 tablespoon fresh rosemary leaves

½ tablespoon finely chopped fresh oregano

¼ cup extra-virgin olive oil

Kosher salt and freshly ground black pepper

1 3½- to 4-pound chicken

½ cup crumbled feta

1 Preheat the oven to 425°F.

2 In a large bowl, combine the eggplant, bread, olives, harissa, garlic, rosemary, oregano, and olive oil and season lightly with salt and pepper. Transfer the mixture to a roasting pan or a large, rimmed baking sheet in an even layer.

3 On a cutting board, using kitchen shears, cut on either side of the chicken's backbone and remove it. Set the chicken breast-side-up and press to lightly crack the breastbone and flatten the breast. Season the chicken all over with salt and pepper and set it on the bread mixture.

Form No. 29819

ANIMAL DOSSIER
Portland, Oregon

NAME Colin

OCCUPATION Chicken

BIRTHPLACE Aliki Farms

SEX Undeclared

BIO

Colin was born and raised on Aliki Farms, just outside of Portland. He spent most of his time outside and could often be found walking around. Or sitting in the pine tree by the barn.

LIVING SITUATION

Colin was free to roam however he pleased around the grounds. In bad weather, the Chicken Coop was available as shelter. He had his own little compartment with a good amount of privacy from the other chickens.

DIET

Squash, Eggplant, Potato Skins, Cracked Indian Corn, Greek Yogurt

Allergies: Avocado

4 Roast the chicken in the center of the oven for about 1 hour, until the skin is crispy and golden and an instant-read thermometer inserted into the thigh registers 165°F, the eggplant is tender, and the bread is lightly toasted in spots. Be sure to lift the bird and stir the mixture occasionally for even browning.

5 Turn on the broiler. Move the chicken to one side and stir the feta into the bread and eggplant. Set the chicken, skin-side-down, on top of the mixture and broil until everything is crispy and lightly browned, being careful not to burn the bread. Flip the chicken so it is skin-side-up, spreading the bread and eggplant mixture all around, and broil for 1 to 2 minutes to recrisp the skin. Cut into pieces and serve.

CHICKEN SHAWARMA WITH TAHINI MAYO

TOTAL: 15 MINUTES ★ SERVES 4

½ cup tahini (sesame paste)
2 garlic cloves, minced
2 tablespoons freshly squeezed lemon juice
½ cup mayonnaise
Kosher salt
2 tablespoons extra-virgin olive oil
1 large onion, cut into thin slivers
2 teaspoons ground cumin
½ teaspoon dried oregano
4 cups shredded leftover chicken, preferably dark meat (about 1 pound)
Hot sauce, chopped lettuce, sliced tomatoes, rice, and warmed pita, for serving

1 In a blender or mini chopper, combine the tahini with ½ cup of water, half of the garlic, and 1 tablespoon of the lemon juice and puree until smooth. Add the mayonnaise and process until creamy. Season with salt to taste.

2 In a large skillet, heat the oil. Add the onion, cumin, and oregano and season with salt to taste. Cook over high heat, stirring, until the onion is lightly charred and just tender, about 5 minutes. Add the chicken, season lightly with salt, and cook, stirring, until heated through.

3 Serve the shawarma with the tahini sauce, hot sauce, lettuce, tomatoes, rice, and pita.

TORTILLA SOUP WITH CHICKEN

TOTAL: 30 MINUTES ★ SERVES 4 TO 6

2 tablespoons vegetable oil

1 medium Vidalia onion, finely chopped

2 large poblano peppers, stemmed, seeded, and finely chopped

2 large garlic cloves, thinly sliced

2 teaspoons ground cumin

Kosher salt and freshly ground black pepper

6 cups low-sodium chicken broth

4 corn tortillas, cut into 1-inch strips

¼ cup fresh cilantro leaves, plus more for garnish

1 pound shredded roasted chicken (about 4 loose cups)

1 cup canned, rinsed, and drained hominy

Sour cream and tortilla chips, for serving

1 In a large pot, heat the oil. Add the onion, poblanos, garlic, and cumin and season with salt and pepper to taste. Cover and cook over medium heat, stirring occasionally, until softened, about 5 minutes.

2 Add the broth and tortilla strips, cover, and bring to a boil. Simmer over low heat until the vegetables and tortilla strips are very soft, about 5 minutes.

3 Add the ¼ cup of cilantro and, using a stick blender, puree the soup until smooth.

4 Add the chicken and hominy and simmer uncovered for 5 minutes longer.

5 Ladle the soup into shallow bowls and garnish with cilantro, sour cream, and tortilla chips.

Make ahead: The soup can be refrigerated overnight. Thin the soup with broth if necessary.

DREAM BUTCHER's

Attention all patrons!
ONE and ALL to see

BUTCHERARIUM

the other half lives
Only the finest

of the **1890s**
PARLOUR

Yes! Oh! And enter
the flavors of the
You are curious how
in their parlours?
purveyors →

TAGLIATA WITH ARTICHOKE SALAD

ACTIVE: 20 MINUTES ★ TOTAL: 50 MINUTES ★
SERVES 4

8 baby artichokes
3 tablespoons extra-virgin olive oil
Kosher salt and freshly ground black pepper
1 boneless strip steak, 3 inches thick
   (about 2 pounds)
4 garlic cloves, halved
4 4-inch sprigs of fresh rosemary
4 4-inch sprigs of fresh thyme
Shaved Parmesan, for garnish

1 Pluck off and discard the outer leaves of the artichokes, revealing a yellow-green core. Using a serrated knife, trim off the top third. Cut each of the artichokes into quarters.

2 Bring a medium saucepan of water to a boil. Add the artichokes and cook for 2 minutes. Drain and pat dry.

3 Transfer the artichokes to a medium bowl and toss with 2 tablespoons of the oil. Season with salt and pepper to taste.

4 Preheat the oven to 400°F and preheat a large cast-iron skillet until very hot.

5 Season the steak with salt and pepper to taste. Add the remaining 1 tablespoon of oil to the skillet and add the steak, garlic, and sprigs of rosemary and thyme. Cook over high heat until the steak is brown and crusty on the bottom and the sides, about 10 minutes. Flip the steak over completely and set the garlic, rosemary, and thyme on top. Add the artichokes to the skillet around the steak.

6 Place the skillet into the oven and roast until an instant-read thermometer inserted into the thickest part registers 135°F, about 20 minutes. Transfer the steak to a cutting board and let rest 10 minutes.

7 Strip the rosemary and thyme leaves from their stems and add them to the artichokes.

8 Thinly slice the steak and arrange it on a platter. Add the artichokes and garnish with shaved Parmesan. Serve right away.

COMMUNAL TABLE ETIQUETTE

Dear Guest,

Thank you for visiting our restaurant. We expect this may not be your first time dining at a communal table. Either way, here is a friendly reminder of some guidelines for making the dining experience pleasant for all those seated together.

1 Space yourselves out. There is no need to sit right next to someone if the table is pretty much empty. Just go to the other end.

2 Please do your best to pretend not to be listening to other people's conversations. In general, we suggest avoiding eye contact or looking at people. The best solution is a smile followed by quickly looking away.

3 Salt, pepper, olive oil, and those little boxes of jelly are meant to be shared. If you are feeling overwhelmed by too much passing-things-to-your-neighbors, just notify our waitstaff. We will bring some more condiments to minimize the need for passing.

4 No matter how nice they seem, please do not request to try a bite of your neighbor's food. Even if they offer. Remember: This person is a stranger.

5   If you need something passed to you, please wait for a pause in your neighbor's conversation before requesting help. (Reminder: As you're listening for this appropriate pause in conversation, avert your eyes in another direction so it doesn't seem like you're eavesdropping.)

6   The communal table is not a place you go to recruit people. For anything.

7   Please don't spoil TV shows for your neighbors or waiters. If you absolutely need to discuss television, we can seat you at a small separate table in the back room.

8   It is important to keep track of whose silverware is whose. If someone uses your fork without realizing it, please avoid confrontation. Just drop the used fork on the ground and we will bring you a fresh fork.

9   Please respect parties of one. It is acceptable to briefly include a party of one in a conversation, but do not bulldoze their dining experience with your questions and stories just because they have no one else to talk to. They may prefer to eat in peace.

10 No telling loud, long stories.

11 Buying alcoholic beverages for people at the other end of the table who you do not know is prohibited. Things can get uncomfortable, so we need to have this rule.

12 No children, sorry. At all.

Portland

— CITY OF ROSES —

STU'S STEWS

FEATURING DONALD

~MENU~

1. MEAT AND POTATERS
2. CURRY CHICKPEA CHICKEN STEW
3. OYSTER STEW
4. IRISH LAMB STEW
5. KALAMATA GOULASH
6. KOREAN SHORT RIB STEW

Stv's
Stews
Featuring
Donald

KOREAN SHORT RIB STEW

ACTIVE: 30 MINUTES ★ TOTAL: 5 HOURS ★
SERVES 6

1 large onion, quartered

3 large garlic cloves, smashed

6 ¼-inch slices of peeled ginger

½ cup soy sauce

½ cup mirin

½ cup unsweetened apple juice

2 tablespoons toasted sesame oil

3 pounds beef short ribs (2½ inches long),
     cut between the bones

2 tablespoons canola oil

4 cups low-sodium chicken or beef broth

1 pound large carrots, cut into 1-inch pieces

1 pound daikon, peeled and cut into 1½-inch
     chunks

6 large fingerling potatoes (about 12 ounces),
     peeled and halved

1 cup vacuum-sealed roasted chestnuts

Steamed short-grain rice and kimchee,
     for serving

1 In a blender, combine the onion, garlic, ginger, soy sauce, mirin, apple juice, and sesame oil and puree until smooth.

2 Pour the mixture into a resealable plastic bag and add the short ribs. Close the bag, press out the air, and let sit at room temperature for 2 hours or refrigerate overnight.

3 Lift the ribs from the marinade, reserving the marinade. Scrape the solid bits off ribs and pat dry.

4 Heat the oil in a large enameled cast-iron casserole over moderate heat. Brown the meat in one batch, turning occasionally, until browned and crusty all over, about 10 minutes. Add the marinade and broth and bring to a boil. Cook over low heat, covered with a slight opening, until the meat is nearly tender, 2 hours.

5 Add the carrots, daikon, potatoes, and chestnuts, tucking them into the liquid as best as possible. Cover and cook until tender, about 1 hour longer, stirring occasionally so the vegetables are mostly submerged.

6 Spoon off as much fat as possible and serve the ribs and vegetables with steamed short-grain rice and kimchee.

Make ahead: The short ribs can be marinated overnight, and the stew can be refrigerated for up to 2 days.

PAELLA VALENCIA

ACTIVE: 20 MINUTES ★ TOTAL: 50 MINUTES ★
SERVES 6

5 cups low-sodium chicken broth

Large pinch of saffron threads

1½ tablespoons extra-virgin olive oil

6 small chicken drumsticks (3 ounces each)

½ rabbit (about 1¼ pounds) cut into 6 pieces
(through the bone; see Note)

Kosher salt and freshly ground black pepper

6 ounces chorizo, halved lengthwise and cut
into ½-inch-thick slices

1 large onion, finely chopped

1 small green bell pepper, finely chopped

2 garlic cloves, minced

1 14-ounce can diced tomatoes, drained

½ teaspoon smoked sweet paprika

1½ cups uncooked short-grain rice, such as
Bomba or Calasparra

1 cup frozen baby lima beans

1 large roasted pepper, cut into ½-inch strips

Lemon wedges, for serving

*Note: Alternatively, omit the rabbit and use slightly
larger chicken drumsticks.*

1 Preheat the oven to 425°F.

2 In a medium saucepan, bring the broth
to a simmer and crumble in the saffron.
Cover and let sit off the heat for 15 minutes.

3 In a 12-inch paella pan or ovenproof
skillet, heat the oil until shimmering.
Season the chicken and rabbit with salt
and pepper to taste and add to the skillet.
Cook over medium-high heat, turning once,
until browned and crusty, about 8 minutes.
Transfer to a platter.

4 Add the chorizo, onion, green pepper,
and garlic to the pan. Cook over medium-
high heat, stirring, until the chorizo has
rendered its fat and the vegetables are
softened, 7 to 8 minutes.

5 Stir in the tomatoes and paprika and
cook, stirring occasionally, until the
mixture is very dry, about 5 minutes.

6 Stir in the rice and lima beans. Nestle
the chicken and rabbit partway into the
rice and arrange the roasted pepper strips
in between. Add the broth and simmer
uncovered over medium heat for 10 minutes,
gently shaking the pan once or twice, but not
stirring. The liquid should be bubbling just
below the surface. Carefully transfer the pan
to the oven and cook, uncovered, until the
liquid is absorbed, about 10 minutes. (The
rice will not be completely cooked.)

7 Carefully transfer the pan to the stove
top, cover with a kitchen towel and lid,
and let sit off the heat for 10 minutes. (The
rice will plump and soften.) Serve the paella
right away, with lemon wedges. Leftover
paella can be formed into patties, breaded,
and fried.

Kath and Dave
- - - - - - - - - - - - -

100% AUTHENTIC SPANISH CUISINE

We hope you enjoy this recipe for
AUTHENTIC paella. As they say in
España: *A comer la paella es un placer
para toda la vida.* I say that as often as
I can, and loudly. Kath and I traveled
extensively and intensely throughout
the northern and southern regions of
Spain. The instructions and amounts
that you see in this recipe are to be
followed precisely.

Love,
Dave

Recommended Online Reviews

Malcolm and Kris
Portland, OR

★ ★ ★ ★ ★

Our students over at the college have raved about this restaurant, so we had to check it out for ourselves. Boy, were they right! Your body will thank you for eating here.

Our very sweet waitress picked out a few things for us to try. It was all very light, but it still felt like real food. The highlight was the quinoa and kale bowl. The dried currant and goji berry salad is also worth trying. And the chipotle tempeh was interesting! Also, we'd recommend getting a side of garlic tahini if you order the sea vegetables.

You should know that after eating here, everyone gets a little gassy. It's normal! There is a beautiful patio in the back of the restaurant where you can fart as much as you please. It's the designated area for farting. You'll love it! The whole place really feels like a community.

Erin
Portland, OR

★ ★ ★ ★ ★

My go-to pick-me-up when I'm feeling low energy is the Green
Dream juice with a double shot of Ginger Bliss. I usually just sit at

KALE AND QUINOA BOWL WITH TOFU AND MUSHROOMS

ACTIVE: 30 MINUTES ★ TOTAL: 45 MINUTES ★ SERVES 4 TO 5

Lay an EGG on it!

QUINOA

1 tablespoon canola oil

1 large shallot, minced (about ¼ cup)

¾ cup quinoa

Kosher salt

VEGETABLES

¼ cup vegetable oil

4 cups trimmed and sliced mixed wild mushrooms (about 8 ounces)

8 ounces firm tofu (not silken), cut into ¾-inch cubes

1 large shallot, minced (about ¼ cup)

2 teaspoons minced fresh, peeled ginger

5 ounces baby kale (about 6 lightly packed cups)

1½ tablespoons soy sauce

1 Make the quinoa: In a medium saucepan, heat the oil until shimmering. Add the shallot and cook over medium heat until softened, about 4 minutes.

2 Add the quinoa and cook, stirring until it's nutty and you begin to hear a popping sound, about 3 minutes. Add 1½ cups water and a pinch of salt and bring to a strong boil. Cover and cook over low heat for 15 minutes, until all the water is absorbed. Let sit off the heat for 15 minutes, then fluff with a fork.

3 Make the vegetables: In a large nonstick skillet, heat 2 tablespoons of the vegetable oil until shimmering. Add the mushrooms and cook over medium-high heat, stirring occasionally, until golden and crisp, about 10 minutes.

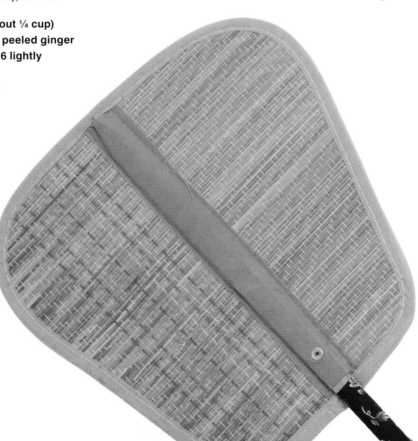

4 Scrape the mushrooms onto a plate and heat another tablespoon of the oil in the same skillet. Add the tofu and cook over moderately high heat, turning occasionally, until browned all over, about 7 minutes.

5 Add the tofu to the mushrooms on the plate and heat the remaining 1 tablespoon of the oil in the same skillet. Add the shallots and ginger and cook over medium-high heat, stirring until fragrant, about 2 minutes. Add the kale and cook, stirring until wilted, about 3 minutes.

6 Return the tofu and mushrooms to the skillet and cook together, stirring, until heated through, about 2 minutes. Add the soy sauce and cook, stirring for 1 minute.

7 Mound the quinoa in bowls and top with the kale, mushroom, and tofu. Serve right away.

Reviewer Submitted Photos

ALEXANDRA'S NO-FUSS LASAGNA

ACTIVE: 45 MINUTES ★ TOTAL: 2 HOURS ★
SERVES 10 TO 12

¼ cup extra-virgin olive oil

1 pound ground beef (chuck or sirloin)

4 large garlic cloves, minced

1 teaspoon dried Italian oregano, crumbled

Large pinch of crushed red pepper flakes

2 tablespoons tomato paste

2 28-ounce cans of peeled San Marzano
    tomatoes, pulsed in a food processor

1 28-ounce can of tomato puree

2 cups low-sodium chicken broth

2 dried bay leaves, preferably imported

2 sprigs of fresh basil

1 tablespoon sugar

Kosher salt and freshly ground black pepper

1½ pounds sweet Italian sausage, casings
    removed

2 pounds fresh ricotta (about 3¼ cups)

½ cup freshly grated Parmigiano-Reggiano

2 tablespoons finely chopped fresh flat-leaf
    parsley

2 tablespoons finely chopped fresh sweet basil

1 pound mozzarella, not fresh, shredded (about
    3 cups)

1 large egg, beaten

1 pound dried lasagna noodles

1 Make the tomato sauce: In a large heavy casserole, heat the oil. Add the ground beef and cook over medium-high heat until no longer pink, about 5 minutes, breaking the meat into large chunks with the spoon.

Alexandra

COOKING FOR ROOMMATES

I don't cook much, but the one thing I know how to make super-well is lasagna. I like to make a huge batch of this stuff on Sunday, stick it in the freezer, and then just pop it in the microwave whenever I'm hungry! It has almost all the food groups—vegetables, starch, and dairy. So pretty healthy. You can add meat if you want to do the entire "food pyramid." And it doesn't need to have meat in it if you're trying to lose weight. And a fun thing to do if you're bringing it to a potluck or a party is take a can of Cheez Whiz and use it to decorate the lasagna with little flowers. Like frosting! You can write your initials. Or if it's someone's birthday you can write a little birthday message on it. Be creative!

2 Add the garlic, oregano, and crushed red pepper flakes and cook until fragrant, 2 minutes. Stir in the tomato paste and cook, stirring, until slightly darkened, about 3 minutes.

3 Add the canned tomatoes, tomato puree, chicken broth, bay leaves, basil sprigs, and sugar. Season with salt and pepper to taste and bring to a boil. Simmer uncovered over medium heat, stirring occasionally, until thickened and reduced to 8 cups, about 1½ hours. Remove the bay leaves and basil sprigs.

4 Heat a large skillet. Add the sausage meat in large pieces and cook over medium-high heat until browned and just cooked through, about 10 minutes. Drain the sausage and break into ½-inch lumps.

5 In a large bowl, combine the ricotta with ¼ cup of the Parmesan, the parsley, and the chopped sweet basil. Add two-thirds of the mozzarella and season with salt and pepper to taste. Stir in the egg.

6 Meanwhile, bring a large pot of salted water to a boil. Add the lasagna and cook, stirring occasionally, until al dente. Drain the noodles and rinse under cold water to stop the cooking. Pat the noodles dry between layers of paper towels, reserving the four best for the top.

7 Preheat the oven to 375°F.

8 Spread 1 cup of the tomato sauce in the bottom of a 9 × 13 × 3-inch rectangular baking dish. Arrange 4 noodles overlapping slightly in the bottom. Spoon half of the ricotta mixture onto the noodles, then spread evenly. Top with half of the sausage and 1½ cups of the sauce. Arrange another 4 noodles on top, followed by the remaining ricotta

mixture, sausage, and another 1½ cups of sauce. Arrange the four best noodles on top and spread with 1½ cups of sauce.

9 Sprinkle the remaining mozzarella and Parmesan on top and bake until the top is browned, crusty around the edges, and bubbling, about 45 minutes. Let the lasagna rest 20 minutes before cutting into squares.

Make ahead: The lasagna can be prepared through step 8 and refrigerated overnight, or it can be baked, refrigerated, and reheated in a 325°F oven.

Malcolm

PRAIRIE HOME COMPANION TAILGATE

My wife Kris and I have been tailgating *Prairie Home Companion* live shows for years now. Years. And every time—*every* time—I'm the idiot stuck doing all of the cooking. Now, how did *that* happen!? And, well, it's not because Kris is lazy. She's a great cook herself, don't get me wrong. No, I'm doing all the cooking at these things because it is the *one time a year* I'll fire up the ol' Crock-Pot and make my Puree Home Comp-Onion. And, let me tell you, my wife is just nuts about it. Just loses her mind over the stuff. I'm starting to think she just wants to go to these live shows for the tailgating food. . . . Nah, not really. She loves the show. Loves Garrison. Maybe a little too much, if you know what I'm getting at. I'm sitting over here starting to think—are you listening to this or not? I'm starting to think my wife loves this soup more than me!

Anyway, this is all just—I'm just joking around with you. You know what I'm thinking? I'm thinking I'll go ahead and give you the secret about how to make the stuff. Don't steal it from me. Or do steal it. Go ahead and take it. That way *you* can do the cooking from now on. I can just kick back on my folding chair and enjoy an ice-cold tea.

PUREE HOME COMP-ONION

ACTIVE: 30 MINUTES ★ TOTAL: 12 TO 18 HOURS, DEPENDING ON THE MACHINE ★ SERVES 6

SOUP

3 large Spanish onions (about 2½ to 3 pounds), halved and thinly sliced (about 12 cups)

4 tablespoons unsalted butter, melted, plus softened butter for spreading

1 tablespoon sugar

2 tablespoons cognac or dry sherry

1 quart beef stock, preferably homemade

1 tablespoon all-purpose flour whisked with 2 tablespoons water

1 bouquet garni made with 1 dried bay leaf, 2 sprigs of fresh thyme, 2 juniper berries, and ½ teaspoon whole black peppercorns, tied in cheesecloth

Kosher salt and freshly ground black pepper

TOPPING

Crusty baguette, sliced ½ inch thick

3 cups loosely packed coarsely shredded Gruyère cheese (about 8 ounces)

1 Heat the slow cooker on high and add the onions, melted butter, and sugar. Toss to coat evenly, cover, and cook on high power until the onions are browned and soft, about 12 hours. Stir the onions several times so they occasionally make contact with the bottom of the slow cooker. Remove the lid, add the cognac, and continue to cook on high power until all the liquid is evaporated and the onions are silky and deep brown, about 2 hours longer, depending upon the machine. Add the beef stock, flour/water mixture, bouquet garni, and salt and pepper to taste, then cover and cook on high power for

2 hours longer, depending upon the machine. Remove the bouquet garni and season the soup with salt and pepper to taste.

2 Preheat the broiler. Butter the bread on both sides and arrange on a baking sheet. Broil in the center of the oven until lightly toasted, turning once. Ladle the soup into ovenproof bowls and set them on a sturdy baking sheet. Add the bread, fitting slices to cover the entire surface. Sprinkle the cheese on the bread and broil in the center of the oven until melted and browned, about 5 minutes. Serve right away.

3 Alternatively, prepare the soup on the stove top. Cook the onions and sugar in the butter in a large deep skillet, covered, over medium heat until softened. Uncover and cook, stirring frequently, until deeply caramelized, about 45 minutes, adding a few tablespoons of water to the pan to prevent scorching. Add the cognac and cook until evaporated. Add flour/water mixture and bouquet garni and simmer for 45 minutes over low heat. Proceed from step 2.

MR. MAYOR'S JAMAICAN JERK CHICKEN

ACTIVE: 30 MINUTES ★ TOTAL: 2 HOURS PLUS
OVERNIGHT ★ SERVES 8 TO 10

6 large garlic cloves
6 scallions, cut into 1-inch pieces
1½ tablespoons fresh thyme leaves
2 Scotch bonnet chiles, seeded
6 ¼-inch pieces peeled fresh ginger
¼ cup distilled white vinegar
2 tablespoons (packed) dark brown sugar
1 teaspoon ground allspice
½ teaspoon freshly grated nutmeg
Kosher salt
2 3½-pound chickens, quartered

1 In a blender, combine the garlic, scallions, thyme, chiles, ginger, vinegar, brown sugar, allspice, and nutmeg and add ¼ cup of water. Puree until smooth.

2 Carefully open the lid, averting your face to avoid fumes, and pour the mixture into a large bowl. Season generously with salt and add the chicken, turning to coat.

3 Refrigerate for at least 4 hours, preferably overnight.

4 Return the chicken to room temperature.

5 Light a grill and oil the grates. Grill the chicken over medium heat, turning occasionally, until lightly charred and an instant-read thermometer inserted into the thigh joint registers 168°F, about 35 minutes. Alternatively, preheat the broiler and set a rack in the lower third of the oven. Broil the chicken on a sturdy pan, turning occasionally, about 40 minutes.

Make ahead: The chicken can be marinated overnight.

Mr. Mayor

*If you can open up your heart
and you can feel the sun
and feel the music
all is good
and all is forgiven*

—King Desmond and the Accelerators

BRIDGETOWN weekly

Free Every Friday Rain or Shine in Portland

MR. MAYOR, OUTED BASS GUITARIST OF REGGAE BAND

▶ SEE PAGE 12

BYOB
bring your own bag

MH: Hi. I'm Marcus Harris.

MH: And I'm Madeline Harris.

MH: And guess what?

MH & MH: We're TWINS!

MH: For years, door-to-door petitioners have been petitioning and *petitioning* to ban the plastic bag in Portland.

MH: And guess what? They did it! Plastic checkout bags are OUT.

MH: You will not find a single plastic bag in a single grocery store in a single neighborhood or area of Portland.

MH: Except for produce bags. The rolled-up clear ones. Those are not banned, but we should please go ahead and ban them. They're really hard to tear apart.

And also you feel guilty about taking a lot of them, so instead you put all of your fruit and vegetables in one bag. And then you feel guilty *again* at the checkout, because the person has to dig through the bag and separate everything, which seems to really irritate them. And the checkout person kind of looks at you. In an annoyed way. The whole thing is very stressful. Let's ban them. Please.

MH: Are you okay?

MH: Yes.

MH: Instead, Portlanders everywhere use reusable canvas bags when shopping. So don't forget your reusable bag when you head to the grocery store!

MH: Reusable canvas bags are not only handy, they also make a statement. The statement is: *I care about the environment.*

GIVE PEAS A CHANCE

MH: Or they can make other statements. They're like a car-free bumper sticker. You may be on a bike, but you still have a way to say, hey guys: I ♥ NEW YORK.

MH: Or, MY OTHER KID IS A CORGI.

MH: I don't get it.

MH: It would have a little corgi illustration on it.

MH: Still don't get it.

MH: It's like I love my corgi so much it's practically my other kid.

MH: You don't have a kid . . .

MH: You've never been to New York City . . .

MH: I had a layover in Buffalo.

MH: That doesn't count.

MH: It's New York. And I loved it.

MH: Your bag is misleading.

CRAIG'S CRAZY GUAC TACS

ACTIVE: 30 MINUTES ★ TOTAL: 45 MINUTES ★
SERVES 4

8 ounces red or green cabbage, finely shredded
(about 6 packed cups)
3 tablespoons freshly squeezed lime juice
Kosher salt and freshly ground black pepper
Extra-virgin olive oil, for brushing
4 small scallions
1 pound red snapper fillets, pin bones removed
2 ripe Hass avocados, mashed
¼ cup chopped fresh cilantro, plus whole
leaves for garnish
12 corn tortillas, warmed
Sliced pickled jalapeños, sliced radishes,
and sour cream, for garnish

1 In a medium bowl, combine the cabbage
with 1 tablespoon of lime juice and a
generous pinch of salt and pepper. Using
your hands, squeeze and massage the
cabbage until just wilted.

2 Light a grill and oil the grates. Brush
the scallions and fish with oil and season
with salt and pepper to taste. Grill over high
heat, turning once, until the scallions are
charred and the fish is cooked through,
about 6 minutes.

3 Chop the scallions and add them to
a medium bowl along with the avocado,
chopped cilantro, and the remaining
2 tablespoons of lime juice and stir to
combine. Season with salt.

4 Serve the fish, cabbage, and guac in
the warm tortillas, garnished with the
jalapeños, radishes, sour cream, and
cilantro leaves.

SLAMBURGER

TOTAL: 40 MINUTES ★ SERVES 4

2 poblano chiles, about 4 ounces each

2 tablespoons vegetable oil, plus more
for brushing

1 large onion, thinly sliced lengthwise,
plus more for serving

Kosher salt and freshly ground black pepper

4 ounces (about 1 cup) shredded Monterey
Jack cheese

3 tablespoons mayonnaise

1 tablespoon Dijon mustard

1 tablespoon ketchup

1 teaspoon Worcestershire sauce

1 pound ground sirloin

1 pound ground chuck

4 large brioche rolls, split

Lettuce leaves and tomato, for serving

1 Roast the chiles over a gas flame, turning, until charred all over. Transfer them to a bowl, cover the bowl with plastic, and let them cool. Then peel, seed, and thinly slice the chiles.

2 In a medium skillet, heat the oil over high heat until shimmering. Add the onion and cook over high heat without stirring, until browned but not softened, about 5 minutes. Add the chiles and cook, stirring occasionally, until charred and tender, about 5 minutes longer.

3 Scrape the mixture back into the bowl, season with salt and pepper to taste, and let cool completely. Stir in the cheese.

4 In a small bowl, combine the mayonnaise with the mustard, ketchup, and Worcestershire sauce.

5 Light a grill and oil the grate.

6 In a large bowl, combine the sirloin and chuck and form into eight 4-inch patties. Make a slight indentation in the center of each patty using your thumb; this will prevent the patties from puffing up when cooked. Brush with oil and season with salt and pepper to taste.

7 Brush the cut sides of the rolls with oil and set aside.

8 Grill the burgers on one side until lightly charred, about 2 minutes. Flip the burgers and mound the chile-onion-cheese mixture onto each and grill for 2 minutes longer for medium to medium-rare meat.

9 Grill the rolls until toasted, about 1 minute, turning once or twice. Stack 2 burgers on each roll and top with lettuce, onion, tomato, and special sauce. Close the burger and serve.

AN OFFICIAL GUIDE TO
FIRE PIT COOKING

◇◇◇◇◇◇◇◇◇◇◇◇◇◇◇◇◇◇◇◇◇◇◇◇◇◇◇◇◇◇◇◇◇◇◇◇◇◇◇

BY MALCOLM AND KRIS

— — — — — — — — —

Making dinner in our backyard fire pit is one of our favorite things to do as a couple. We don't do it as often as we used to, mostly because of our schedules (and sometimes we're just not in the mood). But back in our younger days, we were constantly at it. Just the two of us, the moon, a pot, some tongs, coyote sounds in the distance, and the open flame.

Few things are more exciting than cooking directly over a roaring fire. You think restaurants are romantic with their doilies and tablecloths? You want romance? Try feeding each other under the stars. Directly under them. Candlelit dinners get you hot to trot? Try eating next to a flame so big that you have to take your jacket off and scoot away a little.

Fire pit cooking can get sloppy now and then, but remember: No one is judging. Being dirty is part of the thrill of it. Nobody even needs to know what you're up to. Just keep your voices down.

Safety-wise, it's important to keep in mind that the fire pit can get really hot, and if you're not careful you might get burned. Use protection. Oven mitts, heat-resistant silicone gloves—whatever you have. And keep a bucket of water nearby just in case.

Occasionally while cooking at the pit, one of us might get a little too hot and need to go inside and take a break. Just to cool off. We have realized that it's important that we're comfortable, or else it's just no fun. Generally our rule is: before you stoke, let's talk about how we're both feeling about the temperature situation. If we agree we're ready for another log, let's add one. If either of us is getting sleepy, no more logs. We can just dump some water on the pit and hit the sack.

Just a quick note: Our fire pit is 30 inches in diameter. Original craftsman stone. Hand built by Malcolm.

These are our pit-cooked food recommendations:

SLOPGOALYA

This is a recipe from Kris's Girl Scout days. To make slopgoalya (slop-GOAL-yah), each girl used to put on a blindfold, pick out one can of food from her pantry at home, and bring it to camp. This meant peas, tomato sauce, corn, cooked spaghetti, olives, kidney beans, green beans, mixed beans, black beans, refried beans, chili. Pork and beans. Beans. Anything. You name it.

The next step was to take these cans of everything and dump them into one big pot and stick it in the fire. Once the mixture was bubbling and frothy, we'd each scoop up a heaping portion with our metal camping cups. Mmmm.

The most important ingredient is the blindfold. We still blindfold ourselves to this day and couldn't enjoy slopgoalya without it.

HOT DOGS

There are a million ways to cook a hot dog. You can stick it sideways on the stick and cook it over the fire. Or, for more control, you can carefully pierce it lengthwise right down the middle of the whole wiener. This way you can be sure it won't wobble around or fall off. Nobody likes that. Or you can wrap the hot dog up in foil, pierce it with a stick, and roast it. This provides a steamed effect, which some people like. Or just boil the hot dogs in a pot of beans stuck in the pit. Cut them up first, if desired.

FISH

We have never actually done this before, but we've heard there is a way to wrap a fish in mud, put it in the fire, bake it in there until the mud hardens, take the fish out, crack open the hard mud, and inside the fish is perfectly cooked! The skin keeps it clean, and you just eat the interior meat with your fingers. Everything tastes better if you eat it with your hands, which makes sense. It's primal and you're allowed to have that urge.

HOBO PACKETS/ AKA ANYTHING

It's fun to come up with little names for things. The term "hobo packets" conjures a certain scrappiness, a certain communing with the land.

1. Wrap the food in aluminum foil.
2. Suspend it on a stick (or sticks) and roast it.

S'MORES

We don't eat sugar, but we wanted to quickly note that if you do choose to make s'mores, please be careful. This is Malcolm speaking right now, and I read somewhere, I can't remember where, that burnt marshmallows are extremely dangerous. We're talking *cancer*. From the burnt part.

Peter and Nance
PASTA

Well, I'm back on the Spaghetti Wagon! (This is Peter, by the way. . . . Nance is here, too, but she's quietly reading a book. She is saying hello. Hi, Nance!)

So I'm back on pasta. But in a healthy way. I have learned to indulge my habit in *moderation.* That's the key to a nonabusive relationship with pasta. *Moderation.*

And you know what, it's funny. . . . There are millions and millions and millions of types of pastas out there. There's ravioli. Rigatoni. Mostacholi. Bigoli. Rotini . . . Ricciolini. Fettucini. Linguini. Stringozzi. Conchigliette. Gigli. Fiori . . . Macaroni. Panette. Barbina. Capellini. Pellizzoni. Pici. Ziti. Ciriole. Mafalde. Mafaldie. Lasagna, of course. Pizzoccheri. Tripoline. Cannelloni. Cavatappi. Ditalini. Garganelli. Marziani, which are kind of short spirals. Penne. Pennette. Pennoni . . .

. . . The tennis racket kind . . . Bow ties. Wagon wheels. Seashells. ABCDs. Stars. The kind that is a more *round* bow tie that you'd wear to a less formal event. And those little pieces of pasta-rice. What are those rice ones, Nance? *Orzo.* I can never remember that. *Orzo. Orzo. Orzo.*

All of these different kinds of pasta out there—and what do I like the most? Good ol' boring ol' Spaghetti and Meatballs. I can't help it. Something about the shape? The noodley shape? With meatballs! My mouth, it just: waters. I love it. In moderation, I love it.

Here's the recipe Nance and I like to make together. Just every once in a while . . .

SPAGHETTI AND MEATBALLS

ACTIVE: 45 MINUTES ★ TOTAL: 2½ HOURS ★
SERVES 8 TO 10

¼ cup extra-virgin olive oil

1 very large onion, finely chopped
(about 2 cups)

4 large garlic cloves, minced
(about 2 tablespoons)

¼ cup tomato paste

2 28-ounce cans peeled whole Italian tomatoes,
pureed in a blender (don't buy puree)

3 cups water

1 tablespoon sugar

1 large sprig of fresh sweet basil

2 dried bay leaves

½ teaspoon crushed red pepper flakes

Kosher salt and freshly ground black pepper

1½ cups finely diced white bread (about 2
ounces)

¼ cup whole milk

1 large egg

¼ cup freshly grated pecorino Romano or
Parmigiano-Reggiano, plus more for serving

¼ cup chopped fresh flat-leaf parsley

1 teaspoon minced fresh rosemary

1 teaspoon minced fresh oregano

1 pound ground sirloin

1 pound ground pork

Vegetable oil, for frying

2 pounds dried spaghetti

Crusty bread

1 In a large pot, heat the olive oil over medium heat. Add the onion and garlic and cook over medium heat, stirring occasionally, until softened, about 8 minutes. Scrape half the mixture into a large bowl and let cool.

2 Stir the tomato paste into the remainder of the onion-garlic mixture and cook over medium heat, stirring until the paste takes on a deep rust color, 5 to 6 minutes.

3 Add the pureed tomatoes, water, sugar, basil, bay leaves, and crushed red pepper and season lightly with salt and pepper. Bring to a boil, then simmer over moderately low heat for 1 hour, until slightly reduced.

4 Meanwhile, add the bread and milk to the onions in the bowl and squeeze with your hands, turning the bread into a paste. Add the egg, cheese, parsley, rosemary, and oregano and mix to combine. Add the beef and pork and work until evenly combined. Divide the mixture into 24 scant ¼-cup mounds and, using lightly moistened hands, roll into neat balls.

5 In 2 large skillets, heat ¼ inch of vegetable oil over medium-high heat until shimmering. Add the meatballs and cook, turning occasionally, until golden and crusty all over, about 5 minutes. Using a slotted spoon, transfer the meatballs to a plate and set aside. After the sauce has cooked for 1 hour, add the meatballs and simmer until the sauce is thick and luscious and the meatballs are tender, about 45 minutes longer. Discard the basil and bay leaves.

6 Bring a large pot of salted water to a boil. Add the spaghetti and cook until al dente. Drain the pasta and return it to the pot. Add enough sauce to coat the pasta and cook over medium heat for 1 minute, stirring and tossing. Transfer the spaghetti to a platter and arrange the meatballs all around. Serve with crusty bread and freshly grated cheese.

Make ahead: The meatballs and sauce can be refrigerated for up to 5 days or frozen for up to 2 months.

SHRIMP SAGANAKI

TOTAL: 30 MINUTES ★ SERVES 4 TO 6

¼ cup plus 2 tablespoons extra-virgin olive oil

1 large onion, thinly sliced

Crushed red pepper flakes

1½ pounds ripe plum tomatoes, peeled and coarsely chopped with seeds

1½ pounds cleaned and deveined medium shrimp

½ cup (about 3 ounces) pitted kalamata olives, coarsely chopped

Kosher salt

¼ cup chopped fresh dill

6 ounces Greek feta, crumbled

Crusty bread, for serving

1 In a large skillet, heat the oil over high heat until shimmering. Add the onion and red pepper flakes and cook over high heat, stirring occasionally, until lightly browned, about 5 minutes.

2 Add the tomatoes and cook until softened, crushing with the back of a wooden spoon, about 5 minutes longer.

3 Add the shrimp and olives and season with salt. Cook, stirring occasionally, until the shrimp are curled and cooked through, about 3 minutes.

4 Stir in half the dill and half the feta and cook just until the cheese is heated through, about 1 minute.

5 Transfer to plates, sprinkle with the remaining dill and feta, and serve with crusty bread.

THE GARBAGE AT NICHOLAS'S GREEK RESTAURANT

There was this Greek restaurant in our old neighborhood—so good.

The place was called Nicholas's. That's where I met you—where I met John. In a trash can that was like, *full* of food.

I want Nicholas's!

Remember that great thing they were always throwing out—that, what was that? Shrimp saganaki?

I want shrimp saganaki!

Our new neighborhood—don't get me wrong. Our new neighborhood is great. Plenty of discarded burritos, old vegetables. . . . We're happy with the move. But nothing will ever compare to Nicholas's.

Nothing.

DUMPSTER DIVERS' DINNER PARTY GUIDE

IN THIS DAY AND AGE, THERE IS NO REASON THAT ANYONE NEEDS TO SPEND <u>ONE SINGLE</u> DOLLAR ON FOOD. PEOPLE CALL US "DUMPSTER DIVERS." THAT'S NOT TOTALLY ACCURATE. ~~MOST OF THE~~ MOST OF THE TIME, WE DON'T EVEN HAVE TO GO ALL THE WAY INTO THE DUMPSTERS TO FIND THINGS. SOMETIMES THE MOST AMAZING STUFF IS JUST, LIKE, RESTING AT THE TOP OF THE GARBAGE. AND OTHER TIMES WE FIND PERFECTLY GOOD STUFF JUST CARELESSLY THROWN OUT ON THE STREETS. IN SOME WAYS, WE'RE KIND OF MORE LIKE URBAN <u>FORAGERS</u>.

WE LIKE TO HAVE LITTLE DINNER PARTIES TO SPREAD THE WORD ABOUT THIS WAY OF LIVING. OUR GUESTS <u>CAN'T BELIEVE</u> THAT ALL OF THESE GREAT DISHES WE'RE SERVING HAVE BEEN MADE OUT OF OTHER PEOPLE'S SO-CALLED TRASH. MEG MAKES A GREAT CURRY LENTIL CABBAGE CUMIN STEW SOUP FROM THE GARBAGE CAN BEHIND JEWEL OF INDIA. STUFF LIKE THAT.

IF YOU LOOK IN CHINESE TAKEOUT BAGS, NO ONE EVER USES ALL OF THE SOY SAUCE PACKETS. THEY IGNORE THEM IN THE BOTTOM OF THE BAG. AND A LOT OF TIMES PEOPLE JUST TAKE THE FORTUNES OUT OF FORTUNE COOKIES AND DON'T EVEN EAT THE COOKIE! IT'S EASY TO JUST WRITE YOUR OWN FORTUNES AND STICK THEM BACK INSIDE THE COOKIES. GOOD AS NEW.

WE'VE DEVELOPED A KEEN EYE FOR
DETAIL WHEN DIVING FOR THIS KIND
OF DINNER PARTY. WE RECOMMEND
LOOKING OUT FOR A NUMBER OF THINGS:

SALAD DRESSING BOTTLES.

NO ONE EVER IN THE HISTORY OF
CONSUMERISM HAS EVER USED ALL
OF THE SALAD DRESSING IN THOSE
BOTTLES. THERE'S ALWAYS SOME
LEFT IN THERE. EVEN IF YOU CAN'T
FIND ANY VEGETABLES FOR A SALAD,
YOU CAN USE THE DRESSING FOR
FLAVORING IN STEWS, SOUPS, OR TO
SPREAD ON BREAD (IF YOU CAN FIND BREAD).

* DECORATION *

WE ONCE FOUND A CHINESE LANTERN
THAT WAS A LITTLE RIPPED, BUT NO
ONE COULD NOTICE BECAUSE WE FACED
THE RIP TOWARD THE WALL. IT GOT
A LOT OF COMPLIMENTS. AND LOOK OUT
FOR CHRISTMAS LIGHTS. IT'S AMAZING:
PEOPLE THROW THEM OUT JUST BECAUSE
THEY STOP WORKING. THEY DON'T HAVE
TO BE LIT UP TO BE FESTIVE!

JARS

(FOR USE AS BOWLS, CUPS, PLATES
SUBSTITUTE, OR FOR
GENERAL STORAGE OF STEWS, ETC.)

OUR DINNER PARTIES AREN'T FOR EVERYONE, THOUGH.

SOME OF OUR FRIENDS WILL BE LIKE:
"WHAT CAN WE BRING TO YOUR DINNER PARTY?"
AND WE'LL BE LIKE:
"NOTHING, PLEASE."
AND THEN THEY SHOW UP WITH A PIZZA ANYWAY
AND TRY TO GET US TO EAT THE PIZZA. OR THEY
OFFER TO BUY US SOME GROCERIES OR ~WHATEVER~.
LIKE OUR FRIENDS MARK and TINA. THEY
USUALLY EITHER CANCEL OR BRING US CANNED FOOD
AND LEAVE.

DO YOU HAVE A DOLLAR?

GOOD. THAT'S ALL YOU NEED TO MAKE A MEAL FOR YOURSELF. HERE'S OUR DOLLAR MENU:

$ Pieces of cheese and bread

$ Tacos on Dollar Taco Tuesday at Taco Town

$ Half a slice of pizza

$ Slice of pizza on Dollar Meal Monday at Pizza Face

$ Dollar Beer from 1 to 4 pm at McGinnis Pub on Stark

$ Dollar day-old doughnuts at The Doughnut Hole.

$ Bag of chips and a Coke at Portland Community College Dining Hall. Must ask student to borrow their ID for discount.

$ Bus fare to Mom's house. Anything in the fridge.

SMOKEY BACON PIZZA BIANCA WITH WILD GREENS

ACTIVE: 30 MINUTES ★ TOTAL: 2 HOURS ★ MAKES 2 LARGE PIZZAS

DOUGH

1 teaspoon active dry yeast

Pinch of sugar

¾ cup plus 2 tablespoons warm water (90°F)

2 cups all-purpose flour, plus more for kneading

1 teaspoon kosher salt

Oil for the bowl

TOPPING

4 ounces thick-cut bacon, cut into ½-inch pieces

1 large onion, thinly sliced

1 large garlic clove, thinly sliced

2 tablespoons dry vermouth

½ cup heavy cream

1 sprig of fresh thyme

Kosher salt and freshly ground black pepper

1 tablespoon chopped fresh flat-leaf parsley

4 ounces shredded fontina

4 ounces wild greens, such as arugula, watercress (thick stems discarded), nettles, or purslane (thick stems discarded)

1 tablespoon freshly squeezed lemon juice

1 tablespoon extra-virgin olive oil

½ cup shaved Parmigiano-Reggiano

Olive oil

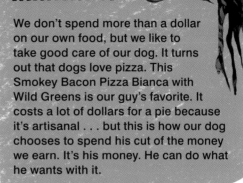

Gutterpunks

We don't spend more than a dollar on our own food, but we like to take good care of our dog. It turns out that dogs love pizza. This Smokey Bacon Pizza Bianca with Wild Greens is our guy's favorite. It costs a lot of dollars for a pie because it's artisanal . . . but this is how our dog chooses to spend his cut of the money we earn. It's his money. He can do what he wants with it.

1 Make the dough: In a large bowl, combine the yeast and sugar. Add the 2 tablespoons of warm water and let sit until the yeast is foamy, about 3 minutes. Add the remaining ¾ cup of water and the flour and salt and stir until a soft dough forms. Turn the dough out onto a floured surface and knead until smooth, adding more flour as necessary.

2 Lightly oil the bowl and return the dough to it. Cover the bowl and let the dough sit in a warm place until doubled in volume, about 1 hour, or refrigerate overnight. Punch down the dough in the bowl, transfer to a cutting board dusted with flour, and cut the dough into 2 equal pieces. Cover with a piece of oiled plastic wrap and let sit at room temperature for 15 minutes.

3 Set a pizza stone in the upper third of the oven and preheat the oven to 500°F, allowing at least 30 minutes for the stone to preheat.

4 Make the topping: In a large saucepan, cook the bacon over medium heat, stirring occasionally, until crisp, about 5 minutes. Using a slotted spoon, transfer the bacon to a paper towel–lined plate and pour off all but 1 tablespoon of the fat from the pan.

5 Add the onion and garlic to the pan, cover, and cook over moderate heat, stirring occasionally, until browned and softened, about 5 minutes.

6 Add the vermouth and cook uncovered, until the vermouth has evaporated. Add the cream and thyme and simmer, uncovered, until the liquid is very thick and the mixture is reduced to ¾ cup, about 5 minutes. Discard the thyme and season with salt and pepper to taste. Stir in the parsley.

7 Working with 1 ball of dough at a time, press or roll it out to a 12-inch circle on a floured surface. Slide it onto a lightly floured pizza peel or an inverted baking sheet.

Spoon the cream mixture on top, followed by the fontina cheese and bacon. Slide the pizza onto the stone and bake until browned and blistered in spots, 6 to 8 minutes.

8 Meanwhile, in a large bowl, toss the greens with the lemon juice and olive oil, and season with salt and pepper to taste. When the first pizza comes out of the oven, mound half the dressed greens on the pizza and garnish with the shaved Parmesan. Cut into wedges and serve right away while the second pizza is cooking.

9 Mound the remaining half of the dressed greens on top of the second pizza when it is done baking, cut into wedges, and serve.

Make ahead: The dough can be refrigerated for up to 3 days; in fact, it takes on a slightly sourdough-like flavor and chewy texture. Return to room temperature before punching down and dividing. The creamy onion topping can also be refrigerated for up to 3 days.

FROM ELLEN'S KITCHEN

BABYSITTER'S MAC AND CHEESE

ACTIVE: 45 MINUTES ★ TOTAL: 2 HOURS ★ SERVES 6

3 tablespoons unsalted butter, plus more
   for the baking dish
3 tablespoons all-purpose flour
2½ cups half-and-half or milk
Pinch of freshly ground nutmeg
Kosher salt and freshly ground black pepper
1 pound sharp cheddar, cut into ½-inch pieces
½ pound Colby-Jack cheese, cut into ½-inch
   pieces
1 tablespoon Dijon mustard
Pinch of smoked paprika
1 pound elbow macaroni
¼ cup freshly grated Parmigiano-Reggiano

1 Preheat the oven to 350°F and generously
butter a 2-quart shallow baking dish.

2 In a large saucepan, melt the butter over
medium heat. When the foam subsides,
add the flour and cook over medium heat,
stirring constantly, for 2 minutes.

3 Add the half-and-half, whisking, and cook
until thickened, about 3 minutes. Add the
nutmeg and salt and pepper to taste.

4 Add half of the cheddar and half of the
Colby-Jack and cook over low heat,
stirring, until the cheese is melted. Off the
heat, stir in the mustard and paprika.

5 Meanwhile, cook the pasta in salted
boiling water until al dente. Drain well,
shaking out any excess water. Return the
pasta to the pot along with the cheese sauce
and the remaining cheese; stir until evenly
combined.

Doug and Claire

ADULT BABYSITTER

Hey, it's Doug. My babysitter Ellen doesn't let me play drums after 9 p.m., which I personally don't think is fair. 9 p.m.? Come on! Right? What am I, a child? I am a man. A full-grown man.

Even though my drum curfew is . . . absurdly outrageous . . . my babysitter can actually be pretty cool sometimes. Overall, I would say that I like her. She watches TV with me. All of the History Channel shows that Claire won't watch . . . like *Car Traders* and *Appalachian Bandits.* And she makes me this macaroni and cheese that is, honestly: so, so, so, so, so, so, so good. So good. So, *so* good. It's all I ever want to eat for the rest of my life. And I hope I live to be, like two hundred—that's how much of this macaroni and cheese I want to eat.

6 Pour the mixture into the prepared dish in
an even layer. Sprinkle the Parmesan over
the macaroni and bake for 45 minutes, or
until bubbling and golden.

7 Let rest for 15 minutes before serving.

Make ahead: The unbaked mac and cheese
can be refrigerated overnight. Return to room
temperature before baking.

DESSERTS

Dessert is so good that it is sometimes tempting to just eat it first. To make it the feature presentation of the dining experience. Who decided that dessert should be the last thing you eat? That it is the *optional* part of the meal? The only reason dessert gets a bad rep is because you typically eat it when you're *not hungry anymore*, which makes it gratuitous and therefore unhealthy.

Maybe we should just have Breakfast, Lunch, and Dessert. Like it gets its own place in the day, so that way you can have more of it and not feel guilty or anything. Thoughts, everyone? Dinner and lunch are mostly made up of the same stuff anyway, right? You have to admit it's a little redundant after breakfast.

This is all just a proposal, but we figured we'd bring it up because the possibility deserves to be discussed. In closing, we would just mention that they serve jalapeño ice cream and bacon chocolate in Portland, so . . . clearly dessert could be its own hearty meal, if we all happened to agree upon this plan.

—FRED AND CARRIE

CACAO BARK

ACTIVE: 20 MINUTES ★ TOTAL: 30 MINUTES ★
MAKES 48 PIECES

9 ounces bittersweet chocolate, finely chopped

1½ cups smoked almonds, roughly chopped
(about 6 ounces)

½ cup cacao nibs

1 Line the bottom of a medium baking
sheet with parchment or wax paper. In
a microwave-safe bowl, melt two-thirds of
the chocolate in 30-second bursts until just
melted but not very hot. Stir until smooth.
Add the remaining chocolate and stir until
melted and cooled to about 92°F. Add two-
thirds of the almonds and two-thirds of the
cacao nibs and stir until evenly coated.

2 Spread the mixture onto the paper-lined
sheet and form it into a thin 12 × 8-inch
rectangle. Sprinkle with the remaining
almonds and cacao nibs. Refrigerate for 10
minutes, or until firm enough to cut.

3 Cut the bark into 48 pieces and transfer
to a plate. Serve chilled or at room
temperature.

Make ahead: The bark can be stored at
room temperature in an airtight container for up
to 4 days or refrigerated for 2 weeks.

Nina
and
Lance
- - - - - - - - -

CACAO

Every couple should have a safeword.
You use it when things go a little too far
in bed and you want to take a break and
just quietly be together. Our safeword,
cacao, was named after a chocolate bar
we saw by the bed. To us, *cacao* means:
I love you, but hands off.

You will love this chocolate bark. You'll
love it so much, but sometimes you
will need a break. You'll want to break
off a piece. And then maybe another
piece. But eventually, you need a break
from the little break off you broke off.
You need to say *cacao* to cacao. And
that's fine. Just enjoy it, but know your
limits. Saying *cacao* is nothing to be
ashamed of.

VARIATIONS

» Crushed pretzels and chopped salted
peanuts

» Dried cherries and chopped toasted walnuts

» Candied orange rind and chopped roasted
pistachios

» Toasted coconut and chopped macadamia
nuts

» Mini white chocolate chips and crushed
candy canes

Brendan
and
Michelle

DURIAN

One of the best things about living here in Portland is having fresh fruit and vegetables delivered right to our door in our weekly Community Supported Agriculture box. We love it. One time, our selection of produce included this exotic specimen all the way from Indonesia: the durian. We had no idea what to do with it. We couldn't even figure out how to cut it open. It turns out that there is actually a great, simple thing to do with confusing or mysterious fruits that arrive in your CSA box. We didn't find out about this recipe until way after the durian flew away.

FRUIT SEMIFREDDO

ACTIVE: 30 MINUTES ★ TOTAL: 5 HOURS ★ SERVES 8

1 large segment of a fresh or frozen durian, pitted (see Note) or ½ cup other fruit, such as mango or pineapple, mixed mango/ banana puree, or pineapple/banana puree
1 teaspoon unflavored gelatin
3 large egg yolks
¾ cup sugar
2 tablespoons freshly squeezed lime juice
3 large egg whites
1 cup heavy cream, chilled

1 Line a 9 × 4½ × 3-inch-deep loaf pan with plastic wrap, allowing at least 3 inches of overhang on all sides.

2 Puree the pitted durian in a food processor until smooth. Scrape the puree through a sieve to remove any tough fibers. You should have about ½ cup of puree.

3 In a small bowl, sprinkle the gelatin over 1 tablespoon of water and let sit until the gelatin has softened, about 5 minutes.

4 In a large bowl set over, not in, a pot with 1 inch of simmering water, whisk the egg yolks together with ½ cup of the sugar. Using a handheld electric mixer, beat on medium speed until the mixture has thickened and an instant-read thermometer registers 160°F, about 6 minutes. Beat in the softened gelatin and the lime juice.

5 Remove the bowl from the heat and beat the mixture on high speed until slightly cooled, 3 to 5 minutes longer. Beat in the durian puree and let cool completely.

6 Using clean beaters, beat the egg whites on high speed until soft peaks form. Continue beating, adding the remaining ¼ cup of sugar 1 tablespoon at a time, until glossy.

7 Using clean beaters, in another bowl, beat the heavy cream until firm peaks form.

8 Scrape both the egg white meringue and the whipped cream into the durian mixture and, using a rubber spatula, fold together until no streaks remain.

9 Fill the prepared loaf pan, gently tapping out any large air bubbles. Fold the plastic directly onto the surface and freeze until firm, at least 4 hours or overnight.

10 Unmold, peel off the plastic, and cut the semifreddo into slices or, using an ice cream scoop, scoop it into balls.

Note: Fresh or frozen durian is available in Asian markets. Some find the flavor and smell of the durian intoxicating, while others are repulsed. Each segment of the fruit has one big pit that easily slips out. The texture of durian is like thick mashed bananas.

Y2K APPLE PIE

ACTIVE: 30 MINUTES ★ TOTAL: 2 HOURS PLUS
4 HOURS COOLING ★ SERVES 12

PASTRY

3¾ cups all-purpose flour, plus more for rolling

1 teaspoon kosher salt

3 sticks (¾ pound) unsalted butter, cut into
½-inch cubes, chilled

¾ cup ice water

Vegetable spray

FILLING

8 to 9 mixed apples (about 3½ pounds), such
as Granny Smith, Golden Delicious, and
Pink Lady, peeled, cored, and thinly sliced

2 tablespoons freshly squeezed lemon juice

1 cup sugar, plus more for sprinkling

⅓ cup all-purpose flour

½ teaspoon ground cinnamon

1 To make the pastry: In a very large shallow
bowl, combine the flour and salt. Add
the butter and, using a pastry blender or
2 table knives, cut the butter into the flour
until the butter pieces are the size of small
peas. Drizzle the ice water on top and stir to
moisten. Don't worry if the dough is dry and
shaggy.

2 Turn the dough out onto a work surface
and press and knead very gently until the
pieces just come together, being careful not
to overwork it. Wrap the dough in plastic and
chill for 30 minutes.

3 Spray a nonstick 15 × 10-inch quarter
sheet pan with vegetable spray.

MEMORABILIA CAFÉ

Hello there! Mr. Mayor here. I'm really
just *so* excited that you've decided
to stop by *Café Y2K*. At *Café Y2K*, we
feature all of the most memorable
memorabilia from the 2000s. We have
preserved this moment in history
through our collection of framed
T-shirts, un-working electronics,
trophies, commemorative knickknacks,
and of course: an autographed Eric
Clapton guitar. All displayed in Plexiglas
boxes with a light shining on them.

American pop culture has changed from
decade to decade since the founding of
this great country, but the one thing that
has been consistently in fashion is, of
course: apple pie. Our apple pie here at
Café Y2K is the best thing on the menu.
The best thing, by far!

The rest of the food is really very bad.

FRIENDSTER
c. 2002 - (World Wide Web)

Friendster is a service that once allowed u
contact other members, maintain those c
online content and media with
ns also used for

4 Lightly flour a work surface and unwrap the dough. Divide it into 2 pieces, 1 piece a little larger with just over half the dough. Roll the larger piece out to a 13 × 18-inch rectangle. Gently ease the pastry into the pan, pressing it into the corners. Trim the overhanging dough to about 1 inch and refrigerate the pan.

5 Roll the second piece of dough out to a 15 × 10-inch rectangle and cut it lengthwise into 12 1-inch-wide strips. Arrange the strips on a lightly floured baking sheet and refrigerate.

6 To make the filling: Preheat the oven to 375°F.

7 In a large bowl, combine the apples and lemon juice. Add the sugar, flour, and cinnamon and stir to combine.

8 Spoon the filling into the dough-filled pan in an even layer. Working with the strips, arrange 4 strips lengthwise over the apples. Arrange the remaining strips crosswise, weaving them between the other strips, cutting and patching to fit.

9 Brush the rim of the pan with water and fold the overhanging dough over the strips along the edge. Crimp decoratively and brush lightly with water. Sprinkle sugar all over the top.

10 Bake the pie in the center of the oven, placing a baking sheet on the bottom rack to catch any spills, until the top is golden and the filling is thickly bubbling through the vents, about 80 minutes. Cover the edges of the crust if they brown too quickly.

11 Cool the pie on a wire rack at least 4 hours before serving.

B&B requirements

Well, hello again, this is Peter and Nance. As you may or may not know, bed and breakfasts in Portland must be inspected and approved by the Portland Bed and Breakfast Bureau before opening. An inspector with a B&B badge comes and visits your B&B to make sure the place has all of the qualifying features:

- *Squeaky staircase*
- *Bedbugs*
- *Inconveniently placed teddy bears*
- *Potpourri*
- *Peeling floral wallpaper*
- *Doilies, everywhere*
- *A smattering of little bars of soap*
- *A smattering of little cookies*

- *Creepy photographs of old-fashioned-looking relatives that kind of watch you*
- *One telephone*
- *Existing but un-working Wi-Fi*
- *A misleading brochure with plenty of unappealing activities*
- *Mandatory 11:00 a.m. checkout. On the dot.*

Our inspector was very impressed by our efficient (and confusing!) solution to the cookie and soap requirements: Nance's Famous Lavender Cookie-Soaps! The recipe follows. If you need to make them soapier, just add soap.

NANCE'S LAVENDER SHORTBREAD COOKIES

ACTIVE: 15 MINUTES ★ TOTAL: 40 MINUTES PLUS
COOLING ★ MAKES 32 COOKIES

1½ cups all-purpose flour

¼ cup plus 2 tablespoons sugar

½ teaspoon salt

1 stick plus 2 tablespoons (5 ounces) unsalted
butter, softened

½ teaspoon pure vanilla extract

1½ teaspoons dried lavender flowers

1 Preheat the oven to 350°F and position a
rack in the center of the oven. Line a large
baking sheet with parchment paper.

2 In a food processor, combine the flour,
sugar, and salt. Add the butter and vanilla
and pulse until evenly moistened. Add
the lavender flowers, and pulse until just
combined. Turn the crumbs onto a sheet of
plastic and press into a disk.

3 Roll the dough out between 2 sheets
of plastic to a rough 8½ × 6½-inch
rectangle. Trim the edges to form an
8 × 6-inch rectangle. Using a straightedge
ruler and a sharp knife, cut the dough into
thirty-two 1½ × 1-inch bars. Set the bars
on the baking sheet, rounding the corners
slightly, and poke 2 or 3 times with a fork.
Freeze just until firm, about 5 minutes.

4 Bake until golden, turning the pan halfway
for even browning, about 25 minutes. Let
cool completely.

Make ahead: The shortbread can be stored
in an airtight container for up to 1 week.

TREAT-YOUR-LOVER-LIKE-YOUR-DOG BONES

ACTIVE: 45 MINUTES ★ TOTAL: 1½ HOURS ★
MAKES 36 SANDWICH COOKIES OR 72 SINGLE
COOKIES

1¾ cups all-purpose flour, plus more for rolling

2 tablespoons unsweetened cocoa powder

2 tablespoons black cocoa (see Note), or
    additional unsweetened cocoa powder

1 teaspoon baking soda

½ teaspoon baking powder

½ teaspoon kosher salt

1½ sticks unsalted butter, softened
    (12 tablespoons)

1 cup sugar

2 ounces unsweetened chocolate, melted
    and cooled

1 large egg

1 teaspoon pure vanilla extract

Crème Filling (recipe follows)

Note: Black cocoa is available from King Arthur or Amazon.

1 Preheat the oven to 375°F. Line 4 baking
  sheets with parchment paper.

2 In a medium bowl, sift the flour with the
  cocoa powder, black cocoa, baking soda,
baking powder, and salt.

3 In a separate bowl, using a handheld
  electric mixer, beat the butter with the
sugar on medium-high speed until creamy.
Add the chocolate, egg, and vanilla and beat
until smooth. Add the flour-cocoa mixture
and beat on low speed until combined.

4 Form the dough into 4 disks, wrap in
  plastic, and chill until firm.

Doug and Claire

TREAT YOUR LOVER LIKE YOUR DOG

Relationships can be tough. When you have been together for a long time (like we have), it's important to come up with new ways to express your affection for each other.

That's never a problem with our dog. We both *love* our dog. We're always so excited to see him when we come home. He's always so earnestly happy when we pay attention to him. It's always just an easy and effortlessly loyal relationship.

So when things get rocky between us as a couple, our trick is to *Treat Your Lover Like Your Dog.* It has worked great for us.

When your lover is being a good boy or good girl, it's important to reward them with treats like this one. Treats reinforce good behavior.

5 On a sheet of floured parchment
  paper, roll one of the disks to ¼ inch
in thickness. Using a 2½- to 3-inch cookie
cutter, stamp out as many cookies as
possible and transfer them to one of the
prepared baking sheets. If the dough gets
too soft, refrigerate to chill it briefly. Repeat
with the remaining dough. Then gather the
scraps and roll out more cookies.

6 Chill the cut cookies for 5 minutes. Bake in batches in the middle and lower third of the oven for about 12 minutes, until puffed and fragrant, shifting the pans from top to bottom and rotating each 180 degrees halfway through. Cool on wire racks.

7 To make sandwich cookies: Pipe or spread 1½ teaspoons of the filling onto half the cookies. Top with the other cookies, pressing to spread the filling out to the edges. Refrigerate the cookies just until set.

Make ahead: **The cookies can be stored in an airtight container for up to 1 week.**

CRÈME FILLING

TOTAL: 15 MINUTES ★ MAKES 2 CUPS
(ENOUGH FOR 36 SANDWICH COOKIES)

8 tablespoons (1 stick) unsalted butter,
  softened
2 tablespoons solid vegetable shortening
1 cup marshmallow fluff
2½ cups confectioners' sugar
Pinch of kosher salt

In a medium bowl, using a handheld electric mixer, beat the butter with the shortening, marshmallow fluff, confectioners' sugar, and salt until fluffy. Transfer to a pastry bag fitted with a ¼-inch plain tip.

NINA'S BIRTHDAY CAKE

ACTIVE: 30 MINUTES ⋆ TOTAL: 1½ HOURS
PLUS COOLING ⋆ SERVES 12

2 cups all-purpose flour, plus more for the pans

2 cups sugar

½ cup unsweetened Dutch process cocoa
   powder

¼ cup black cocoa powder (see Note)

1 teaspoon baking soda

1 teaspoon baking powder

½ teaspoon kosher salt

4 tablespoons unsalted butter, softened,
   plus more for the pans

½ cup vegetable oil

2 large eggs

¾ cup buttermilk

2 teaspoons pure vanilla extract

¾ cup warm brewed coffee (not hot)

1 tablespoon small nonpareils

Rich Pudding Frosting (recipe follows)

*Note: Black cocoa is available from King Arthur
or Amazon. Alternatively, omit the black cocoa and
use ¾ cup unsweetened Dutch process cocoa.*

1 Preheat the oven to 350°F. Line the
bottoms of two 8-inch round cake pans
(2 inches deep) with parchment paper. Butter
the paper and sides of the pans and dust
with flour, tapping out the excess.

2 In the bowl of a standing electric mixer
fitted with a wire whip, gently whisk
together the flour, sugar, cocoa powders,
baking soda, baking powder, and salt.

3 In a medium bowl, whisk the softened
butter with the oil, eggs, buttermilk,
and vanilla.

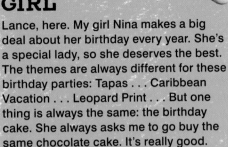

Lance

MY BIRTHDAY GIRL

Lance, here. My girl Nina makes a big
deal about her birthday every year. She's
a special lady, so she deserves the best.
The themes are always different for these
birthday parties: Tapas . . . Caribbean
Vacation . . . Leopard Print . . . But one
thing is always the same: the birthday
cake. She always asks me to go buy the
same chocolate cake. It's really good.
Just like my girl. She's a good girl.

4 On low speed, add the egg mixture to the
flour mixture in the electric mixer bowl,
beating until smooth.

5 On low speed, add the coffee in a thin,
steady stream and beat until combined,
scraping the bottom and sides of the bowl.

6 Divide the batter between the pans and
bake in the center of the oven for 35 to
40 minutes, or until springy and a toothpick
inserted into the center comes out clean.

7 Let the cakes cool in the pans on a wire
rack for 20 minutes, then turn out onto the
rack to cool completely. Peel off the paper.

8 Using a serrated knife, shave off a tiny
bit of the tops to create a slightly flat top
(don't take off too much, just the top of the
dome).

9 Transfer the trimmings to a food
processor and pulse to fine crumbs.
Add the nonpareils and pulse once or twice
to combine.

10 Carefully slice the cake layers horizontally in half so you have 4 even layers.

11 Set 1 layer on a plate and, using the pastry bag fitted with a ½-inch star tip or a sturdy zip-closure plastic bag with a corner cut off, pipe a scant ½-inch layer of frosting (about ⅔ cup) onto the cake layer. (Piping the frosting onto the cut layers as opposed to spreading in large dollops helps avoid tearing the cake and pulling up crumbs.) Then, using an offset spatula, spread the piped frosting evenly, trying to avoid pulling up too many crumbs.

12 Repeat with the remaining layers, reserving the best layer (inverted bottom) for the top of the cake.

13 Pipe all of the remaining frosting onto the top layer and around the sides of the cake, using the offset spatula to spread the frosting evenly. Using your hands, press the cake crumbs onto the sides of the cake.

14 Refrigerate for at least 1 hour. Cut into slices and serve.

Make ahead: The frosted cake can be refrigerated in an airtight container for up to 4 days.

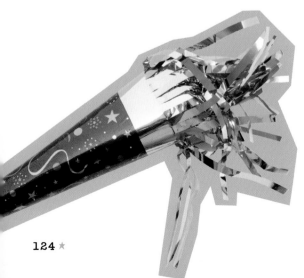

RICH PUDDING FROSTING

TOTAL: 30 MINUTES PLUS COOLING ★ MAKES 4 CUPS (ENOUGH FOR ONE 4-LAYER 8-INCH CAKE)

2 cups whole milk
1 cup heavy cream
⅓ cup cornstarch
1 cup sugar
2 tablespoons black cocoa (see Note)
½ teaspoon kosher salt
8 ounces bittersweet chocolate, finely chopped
6 tablespoons unsalted butter, cut into cubes
1 teaspoon pure vanilla extract

Note: Black cocoa is available from King Arthur or Amazon. Alternatively, use 2 tablespoons unsweetened Dutch process cocoa.

In a large saucepan, combine the milk, cream, cornstarch, sugar, cocoa, and salt and whisk until completely smooth. Cook over moderate heat, whisking constantly, until very thick and bubbling, about 5 minutes.

Off the heat, add the chocolate and whisk until melted and smooth. Whisk in the butter and the vanilla and scrape the pudding into a bowl.

Press a sheet of plastic wrap directly onto the surface and refrigerate until chilled and firm, at least 2 hours.

Transfer the pudding to a large pastry bag fitted with a ½-inch star tip. You could also use a zip-closure plastic bag with a corner cut off.

Make ahead: The pudding can be refrigerated in an airtight container for up to 3 days before spreading.

04

DRINKS

The Drinks Industry is actually a significant part of the Portland economy. There are tons of interesting bars, coffee shops, and microbreweries all over the city. People work as baristas by day and mixologists by night. So much attention and care is put into the presentation of these drinks--it's almost like they are their own official course of the meal.

Coffee is a really big deal in Portland. There are competitions between baristas here. Like the Olympics of who-can-brew-the-best-coffee-the-fastest and execute the most impressive latte art. And we're not talking hearts or cute little milk-waves--Portland lattes feature things like a skull and crossbones or a portrait of someone who looks like they're maybe supposed to be Prince.

It's actually kind of strange how many great coffee shops there are in Portland. How many coffees can the whole city possibly drink in one day to sustain so many great places? Admittedly, people kind of work in the coffee shops, too . . . and not just the baristas. The people who set up their offices there and have meetings or write all day. To be able to set up shop in a coffee shop like that, someone should probably pay a rent of at *least* one coffee or non-caffeinated beverage per three-hour stay. Right? That sounds fair. There should be someone whose job it is to enforce the rent. Like the landlord of the coffee shop office. That should be a job they create in Portland.

And one great thing about bars here: There's a rule where a bar has to also serve food. That's how it should be everywhere!

—FRED AND CARRIE

Marty from Celery, here. I'm pleased to report that America's favorite vegetable is back on the table. Of the many, *many* uses for my product, the classic Bloody Mary is a personal favorite. It is a refreshing pick-me-up that will quench your thirst and fill you up if you're hungry. It's almost like a boozey soup—just delicious.

I'd warn you that certain bartenders will mistakenly put pickles, beets, or carrots in your Bloody Mary. These fools are simply being careless or sloppy. No need to be upset or confrontational with them. When you order, just politely and clearly specify that you want an authentic Bloody Mary, which is made with *celery*.

If you're looking for a tasty snack to accompany your Bloody Mary, don't forget the playful and delicious Ants on a Log. Here's the recipe for that:

ANTS ON A LOG

FOR THE LOG
One stick of celery, washed and
   carefully dried.
Spread peanut butter across the
   celery. Peanut butter can be chunky
   or smooth, depending on your
   personal preference. (I'm a smooth
   man, myself.)

FOR THE ANTS
The "ants" are just California Sun-
   Dried Raisins, *America's favorite
   fruit product.*

Place the "ants" along the "log"
as if they are marching in a
single-file line from one end
of the log to the other. Like
they're on their way to work. And
voilà: you have Ants on a Log.

Please enjoy your celery!

BLOODY MARY

TOTAL: 5 MINUTES ★ MAKES 4 LARGE DRINKS

4 cups tomato juice, chilled

2 tablespoons freshly squeezed lemon juice

1 to 2 tablespoons prepared horseradish

1 teaspoon Worcestershire sauce

Freshly ground black pepper

Tabasco sauce

6 ounces vodka

Ice

4 celery stalks and 4 lemon wedges,
    for garnish

1 In a large pitcher, combine the tomato juice, lemon juice, horseradish, and Worcestershire sauce and season with pepper and Tabasco sauce to taste. Stir in the vodka.

2 Fill 4 Collins glasses with ice. Pour the drink over the ice and add a celery stalk and lemon wedge to each glass.

Coffee LAND!

コーヒー天国〜

VISIT PORTLAND, OREGON, USA: COFFEE LAND!

アメリカ合衆国のオレゴン州、ポートランド市を訪問
〜いわゆるコーヒー天国〜

"You'll Just Love How They Roast the Beans Here!"

Coffee Land!

▶ **Home of World-Champion Baristas**
ワールドチャンピオンのバリスタの街

▶ **Five-Star Latte Art**
5つ星ラテ・アート

▶ **AND COFFEE IN SO MANY SIZES:**
コーヒーのサイズも豊富

Regular 普通

Smaller もっと小さい

Smaller もっと小さい

Smaller もっと小さい

Smaller もっと小さい

Smaller もっと小さい

BURN-YOUR-FACE-OFF MARGARITA

ACTIVE: 5 MINUTES ⋆ TOTAL: OVERNIGHT ⋆
MAKES 2 DRINKS

Ice

3 ounces Chile-Infused Tequila (recipe follows)

2 ounces Cointreau or triple sec

1½ ounces freshly squeezed lime juice

Thinly sliced lime and red chile, for garnish
 (optional)

1 Fill a cocktail shaker with ice. Add the
tequila, Cointreau, and lime juice. Cover
and shake vigorously until the shaker is
frosty, about 30 seconds.

2 Strain into a chilled margarita glass.
Spear the lime and chile slices on a
cocktail pick and garnish.

CHILE-INFUSED TEQUILA

ACTIVE: 5 MINUTES ⋆ TOTAL: 8 HOURS OR
UP TO 2 WEEKS ⋆ MAKES 1 (750 ML) BOTTLE

2 red cayenne chiles, halved lengthwise

1 750 ml bottle of tequila, silver or white
 recommended

Drop the chiles into the bottle, seal, and let
sit at room temperature until infused with
heat and flavor, at least 8 hours or up to 2
weeks.

Toni and Candace

BURN-YOUR-FACE-OFF MARGARITA

Feminism is all about "giving reviews of things." The suffragette movement was all about women demanding the right to vote—that's giving a *good review* of the president. As women, we refuse to allow our bodies to be *reviewed.* We issue a *very bad review* of the Patriarchy (one star, the lowest rating anyone can get).

Reviews are an expression of our voice as women and, trust us, they go A LONG WAY. We learned this from our friend and customer, female tennis star Martina Navratilova. Martina gave a very good review of our store, *Women and Women First.* It can be seen on display on our checkout counter. Our store was popular before, but now it is more popular than ever because of her very flattering and positive review.

To Martina, we would like to say: Thank you for the inspiration and thank you for introducing us to those Burn-Your-Face-Off Margaritas. We raise them in a toast to you, a true champion of feminism. Both Martina and the margaritas get a five-star review. Which is the highest rating on the star scale. That's as many as you can give. We'd give more, but it doesn't work that way.

RECOMMENDATIONS

STAFF FAVORITES

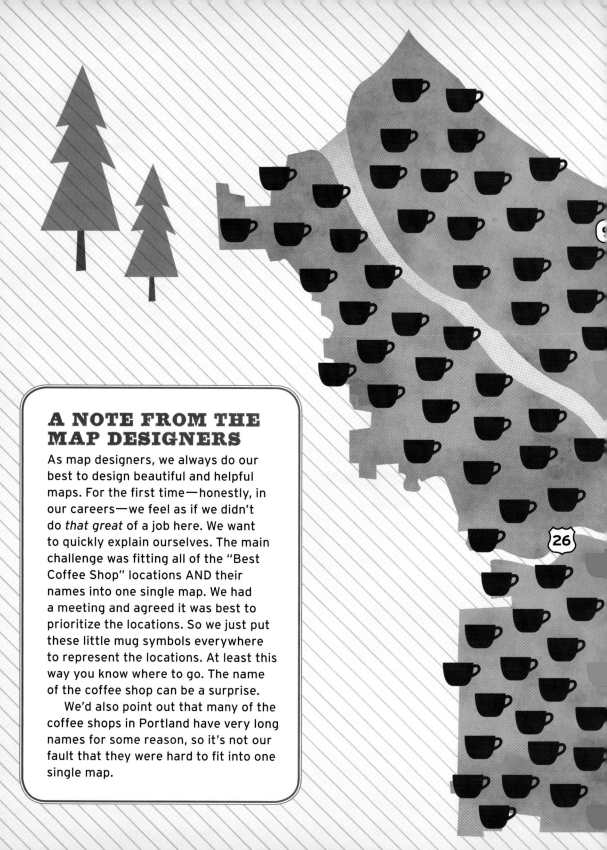

A NOTE FROM THE MAP DESIGNERS

As map designers, we always do our best to design beautiful and helpful maps. For the first time—honestly, in our careers—we feel as if we didn't do *that great* of a job here. We want to quickly explain ourselves. The main challenge was fitting all of the "Best Coffee Shop" locations AND their names into one single map. We had a meeting and agreed it was best to prioritize the locations. So we just put these little mug symbols everywhere to represent the locations. At least this way you know where to go. The name of the coffee shop can be a surprise.

We'd also point out that many of the coffee shops in Portland have very long names for some reason, so it's not our fault that they were hard to fit into one single map.

PORTLAND'S
Best Coffee Shops

205

84

COFFEE SHOP MANIFESTO

THE FOLLOWING IS A MANIFESTO AGAINST CUSTOMERS AND MANAGEMENT INTENDED TO PROTECT US AS THE ARTISTS THAT WE ARE.

— THE SOCIETY OF BARISTAS OF PORTLAND, OREGON

- NO "CHATTING" WHEN YOU COME UP TO THE COUNTER
- NO BATHROOM USE BEFORE YOU ORDER
- NO QUESTIONS
- DO WE HAVE ANYTHING SWEET? NO. WE ONLY HAVE ONE LITTLE SQUARE SCONE-Y THING.
- THIS IS NOT YOUR OFFICE. DO NOT "SET UP SHOP" or "CAMP OUT" HERE WITH YOUR LAPTOP. YOUR SCREENPLAY IS BAD. WE CAN TELL.
- NO CELL PHONES. SHUT YOUR MOUTH.

- KNOW WHAT YOU WANT TO ORDER BEFORE APPROACHING THE COUNTER.
- THE OPEN MIC NIGHT IS NEVER.

- TAKE OFF YOUR SUNGLASSES WHEN ORDERING.
- DON'T ASK US WHAT MUSIC IS PLAYING RIGHT NOW. THIS IS A COFFE SHOP, NOT A RECORD STORE.

- THE WI-FI PASSWORD IS: LEAVE. GO!

- BUS YOUR OWN TABLE. WE'RE BUSY.

- THE COFFEE IS NEVER TOO HOT. IF YOU SPILL IT, THAT WAS YOUR FAULT.

- UNATTENDED CHILDREN WILL BE ASKED TO LEAVE.

- DO NOT ASK WHAT IS GOOD. IT IS ALL GOOD.

- OPEN YOUR MOUTH! ALSO SHUT UP! GET OUT!

TWO-BANANA DAIQUIRI

TOTAL: 10 MINUTES ★ SERVES 4

2 large ripe bananas

3 ounces light rum

2 ounces freshly squeezed lime juice

1 ounce St-Germain liqueur or crème de banana, triple sec, or ginger liqueur

1 ounce simple syrup (see Note)

2 cups ice cubes

Lime and banana slices, for garnish

1 In a blender, combine the bananas, rum, lime juice, St-Germain liqueur, and simple syrup and puree until smooth. Add the ice cubes and puree until frosty and smooth.

2 Pour into tall glasses and garnish with lime and banana slices.

Note: To make your own simple syrup, stir together equal parts sugar and water over medium heat until dissolved. Let cool, then pour into a glass jar, and seal. Can be stored at room temperature almost indefinitely.

Peter and Nance
- - - - - - - - - - - - - - - -

IT TAKES TWO BANANAS

Well, I came here on this day.
'Cause you are my man.
And we've got a love worth saving.
And we need to make a plan.
I was walking down the beach
and a wise man said to me that "it takes two bananas—to make a daiquiri."
Two bananas . . .
The two bananas represent a Man and a Woman
Me and You
Together we make the perfect daiquiri.
. . . it takes two bananas to make a daiquiri
I thought that I was whole
with my lime juice and my rum
a maraschino cherry
and just one banana chunk.
I was blind you see
and I hear what you're sayin' to me:
that our two bananas make a better recipe.
And when you add a third banana
the drink just gets too sweet!
You can't even get it through the straw
It just ain't no kind of treat.
'Cause it takes two bananas
to make a proper daiquiri . . .
Two bananas
to make a proper daiquiri . . .
Two bananas to make a banana daiquiri!
Two bananas for a daiquiri!
Two bananas for a daiquiri!
Two bananas for a banana daiquiri!

—The Bahama Knights

The Portland
Milk Advisory Board

Hi, we're Royce and Alicia from the Portland Milk Advisory Board.
[Before we go any further, we just want to be clear about something, right up front: at the moment, Alicia is back to being the boss. So you know who these recommendations are coming from: Alicia.]

We're here with an update about the latest important changes in the Milk Industry!

We are all familiar with the drawbacks of traditional cow's milk, so we recently issued a series of recommendations for alternative, supposedly better milks. As it turns out, those milks were *not* actually better. In fact, many of them (i.e., *all* of them) had occasionally serious side effects. The milks and accompanying side effects are listed here. Please carefully read this list and go to the doctor if you're feeling weird.

Sorry about that, everybody! But don't be mad at us. Research is hard.

ALTERNATIVE MILKS & THEIR SIDE EFFECTS

	TYPE OF MILK	SIDE EFFECTS
⚠	**Berry seed milk**	*stomach/teeth/face discoloration*
⚠	**Cashew milk**	*numbness of the thumbs*
⚠	**Cookie milk**	*immediate sleepiness*
⚠	**Garlic milk**	*uncontrollable urges to consume pasta*
⚠	**Hemp milk**	*creates a natural rope in your stomach*
⚠	**Octopus milk**	*it's just ink; no side effects*
⚠	**Onion milk**	*no side effects, but too expensive*
⚠	**Radish milk**	*chronic blandness*
⚠	**Sesame milk**	*chronic unnecessary secret-keeping*
⚠	**Sweet potato milk**	*holiday-themed hallucinations*
⚠	**Unregulated goat milk (we didn't know)**	*attraction of flies to the head*
⚠	**Unpasteurized raw milk**	*technically considered a solid food; side effects vary*
⚠	**Zucchini milk**	*delusions of hearing loss (but hearing is actually fine)*

MILK

PLEASE DRINK RESPONSIBLY

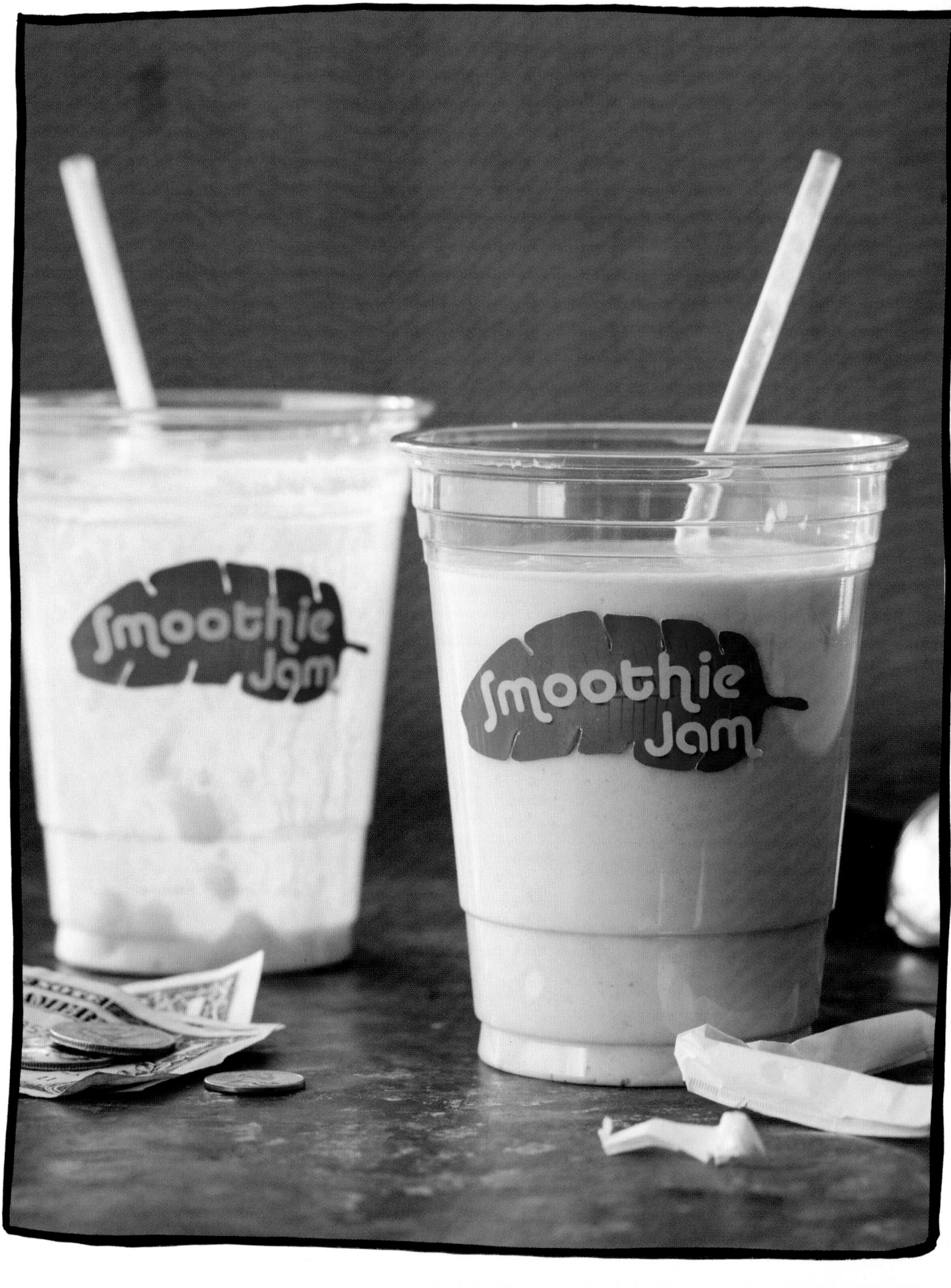
Smoothie Jam
Smoothie Jam

Joaquin

SMOOTHIE JAM

People ask how I got this body, and I usually keep the whole secret to myself. It's kind of just my thing, you know? No need to tell everyone about it. But between us, the secret is: stick to a routine. Maintaining a routine is the key to total health and fitness.

Every morning my watch goes off, I get out of bed, walk out the door, walk down the street, walk all the way to the gym, and work out with my trainer, Billy. After our workout, I say goodbye, take a shower, walk down the stairs, and walk to work. (I got a new watch with a step counter so I can keep track of all of my walking.)

I work at Smoothie Jam, a smoothie lab in the Pearl district. At Smoothie Jam, our smoothies are full of essential nutrients—vitamins and enzymes and protein. And the best part is that they are enjoyable. Employees are allowed to enjoy one free smoothie every day. I drink my smoothie at 11 a.m., when my watch goes off. Here's the recipe I make on Mondays, to start the week off on the right foot.

MANGO LASSI SMOOTHIE

ACTIVE: 10 MINUTES ★ TOTAL: 1 HOUR
(OR 10 MINUTES) ★ MAKES 2 SMOOTHIES

2 cups ripe 1-inch mango chunks
1 cup plain whole or reduced-fat yogurt
   (not Greek style)
1 cup whole or reduced-fat milk
3 tablespoons agave syrup
1 teaspoon pure vanilla extract
Pinch of cardamom

1 Place the mango chunks on an uncovered plate and freeze until just solid, about 1 hour (alternatively, use frozen mango chunks).

2 Place the mango, yogurt, milk, agave, vanilla, and cardamom in a blender and process until smooth. Pour into tall glasses and serve with straws.

GAHVIN'S RECORDING STUDIO DREAMS

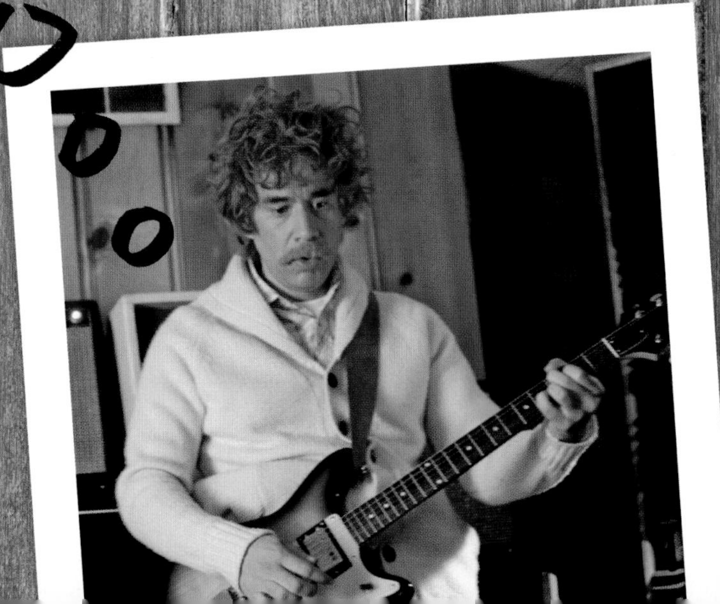

RULES FOR DRINKS
AT MY RECORDING STUDIO

No drinks of any kind near the Mackie mixing board. (Except for maybe a mug of herbal tea way, way on the side, but not above the hard drive.)

Coffee is to be served in mugs that have obviously been collected on the road and have a certain comedic value to them, but at the same time, not ironic. For example: a mug from the Hoover Dam gift shop. Reaction from drummer as he takes a sip of coffee: "You know, it's actually pretty amazing. The Hoover Dam."

Ingredients listed on cans of diet soda are to be discussed at length while mixing a record. You must read them out loud with an incredulous tone.

There's a bowl of water by the door for your lovable, but slow, quiet dog.

Glass bottles are great for percussion overdubs. That's what they used on *Pet Sounds*.

WOMEN'S TEA

Candace: This Khappu Jiu Jiu Jiu Jiu tea is meant for women *only.* If you're a man, we are *not* sorry, but this tea is not for you. Ever. (P.S. to the men: If you try it, that's your own fault. You were warned and we are not to blame.)

I'm talking only to the women from now on. I recommend Khappu Jiu Jiu Jiu Jiu Tea to every woman. You and You and You and You.

I drink as much of this tea as I can. It tastes like charcoal. It also clears out my tear ducts and keeps my skin nice and dry.

Toni: She drinks a lot of it.

CANDACE'S KHAPPU JIU JIU JIU JIU TEA

IMPORTANT! PORTLAND HEALTH BUREAU WARNING:** We're pretty sure this tea is HIGHLY TOXIC for both men *and* women. DO NOT CONSUME. (Also, please, let's keep this between us. We tried to explain to Candace the health risks of her "tea," but let's just say it didn't go over well. At all.)

TOTAL: 1 TO 40 MINUTES ★ SERVES 1

1 cup water
Some metal or a tin object
(Something like an old key or keychain or padlock. It should NOT be rusty. Just sort of old-looking.)
Pinch of dry *khappu jiu*

1 In a medium saucepan, bring the water to a boil. Put the metal or tin object into the boiling water. For those women who are more iron-deficient than the rest of us, let the metal steep for up to 40 minutes.

2 Decant the hot liquid into a Mason jar.

3 As the water cools, add the pinch of *khappu jiu* and stir to combine. It smells a little like soot. I'm hooked.

A Mixologist's Guide to Ice

A Mixologist walks into a bar.
Bartender says, "What can I get you?"
Mixologist says, "A tall glass of water, four hours, and your freezer."

Ice is the most basic ingredient that distinguishes mixology from bartending. Think about it. You could order a vodka cranberry in an everyday glass of melty cubes at some sports bar. But if the same drink is presented over ice shaped like a tennis ball (maybe with a little salted cumin around the rim of the glass), the experience of drinking it is elevated. This is the science—and art—of mixology.

The origins of modern mixology can be traced back to ancient apothecaries. Back in those times, these wizard-esque guys mixed up all kinds of potions that people drank like medicine. We use the exact same techniques to this day, but we add booze. For instance, we all love egg whites in our cocktails, that's a given. Well, there is an old-fashioned thing where you whip egg whites with a pinecone. This is, by far, the best way to make egg whites really light and frothy. Plus, the cone infuses the foam with subtle pine undertones. The pine pairs very nicely with citrus concoctions, such as the classic Blood Orange Fizz. And, of course, it is a crucial feature of winter drinks like my Winter Horse Barn Nog.

The pairing of an elixir with ice cube is intentional and essential. Here is a basic guide, though it is actually way more complicated than this.

ICE BLOCK
◇ Just something to have around. You can rest it right on the bar. As needed throughout the evening, you chip it into smaller cubes with a Bartender's Ice Pick. Can also be shaved with an ice shaver for shaved ice.

LEGO-SHAPED ICE
◇ Nice to have around in case a kid shows up. I drink pop with these every once in a while. Just a nostalgia thing, I guess.

SHAVED ICE
◇ Delicate. Pairs well with a floral palette. Good with gins and elderflower liqueur.
◇ There is a way to rest shaved ice on top of a drink—on the surface of the liquid. You can curl it up into a flower-like ice design. You just have to be really careful and use tweezers.

LARGE ICE CUBE

◇ Hints of tobacco or coin flavor. Hearth-like.

◇ Use for whiskey and for milky drinks, such as Milk Punch.

ICE BALLS

◇ The classic ice ball is the size of a tennis ball. But you can also do Ping-Pong size ice balls and put three to four of them in a drink at once. This looks really cool if the drink is a fluorescent color, such as chartreuse. This can be achieved via food coloring. (Best served with a light under it.)

◇ Egg white cocktails should definitely be served "up" with a ball.

SNIFTER-SHAPED ICE

◇ These are hard to make and sort of hard to drink out of, but they work really well with top-shelf liquors. They keep the elixir cool and pristine, without interfering with the taste. Also, they melt fast, so be sure to drink quickly.

CRUSHED ICE

◇ Best with mint, cucumber, and bananas.

◇ Recommend infusing crushed ice with jalapeños or olive oil.

DECORATIVE ICE

◇ Sort of stupid, but you can freeze little surprises in ice cubes, if you feel like it. Like small flowers or raspberries.

◇ One time, on a whim, I froze some Gummi Bears in ice cubes (which, I know, is so dumb; I was just messing around). They got written up in Bridgetown Weekly, in last spring's "Portland Mixolog-off" edition. They won third place in the ice category. For whatever reason, I guess. Now I have to make them constantly because people like them, apparently.

ACORN-SHAPED ICE

◇ Nutty or earthy drinks.

◇ I use these for any kind of nog. They interact with the nog in a way that is distinct. It's hard to put a finger on exactly what it is, but it's something about the melt ratio of the acorn shape in relation to the nog.

EGG-SHAPED ICE

◇ Mellow drinks that taste almost like nothing but are buttery. A buttery nothing, with a honey aftertaste.

◇ Serve drink with a single, big egg-shaped piece of ice.

BRUNCH

05

Brunch is a weekly ritual here in Portland, the grand finale of meals on the final day of the week. Everyone believes that it is a big deal. Everyone. Every-single-Portlander. We all stand together in agreement--single-file, in one, occasionally unruly line.

Be prepared for the line. There is no way to beat the line. You might think you have a strategy to defeat it, but you don't. You might think that arriving at the restaurant two hours before it opens will get you in without delay. Right? . . . Wrong. The line will already be there.

Then, when you've finally finished your meal at like 3 p.m., you'll notice that there is NO LINE outside the restaurant at this time. So you come back next week at 3 p.m.-- and, sorry buddy, everyone noticed the 3 p.m. thing, too. And they're all waiting in line now.

The one thing about the line though--the unspoken or maybe unnoticed thing--is that it can actually be not-so-unpleasant. We all get eyeroll-y about the line, but that's part of the ritual: complaining about it. Sometimes the line is secretly kind of fun. The entire city is out on the street together, standing around and talking. Disheveled couples in the earliest stages of getting to know each other, kids making new kid-friends, bikers chatting with drivers, jugglers taking a break for a minute. The line can be the whole joy of going to brunch.

—FRED AND CARRIE

Fisherman's Porch

Welcome to Fisherman's Porch. Among many menu items you will find our famous Marionberry Pancakes.

Our marionberries are hand-picked on Sauvie Island during the height of the harvest—the brief window between July 30 and August 2— that's when you have to pick them to get the pancakes right. We harvest our marionberries from the shady bottom third of the berry bush, to avoid oversweetening by the sun. The highly skilled hand-pickers we employ know exactly how to separate berry from bush without damaging the tender and vulnerable flesh of the fruit. Each berry is then carefully and individually packaged and transported by cart to our berry vault in Northeast Portland. There the berries are properly aged before being transported by cart to our kitchen.

(Please allow additional 50 to 60 minutes if ordering the pancakes due to preparation needs.)

BRUNCH DISHES

Marionberry Pancakes
A stack of four cornmeal pancakes to
hand-picked Sauvie Island marionber

Bird in a Grilled Cheese Nest
A Fisherman's Porch favorite! A three
grilled cheese nesting a truffled frie
11

Cream Cheese–Filled Pumpkin French Toast
We recommend sharing with the w
as "table toast!"   9.5

Fried Egg Sandwich
Uncle Jack's Sunday Breakfast. Se
stone-ground-wheat English muff
Vegetarian option not available. N
11

Red Flannel Hash
A perfectly round poached egg
served atop a hash of beets, saln
fingerling potatoes   10.5

DRINKS

Garden Vegetable Blood
Spicy Kimchi Bloody Ma
Mimosa   9
Blood Orange Mimosa
Bottomless Coffee   3
Tea   3

CREAM CHEESE-FILLED PUMPKIN FRENCH TOAST WITH PECANS

TOTAL: 30 MINUTES ★ SERVES 4

½ cup pecan halves
4 ounces cream cheese, softened
1 tablespoon confectioners' sugar, plus more for dusting
¾ cup canned pumpkin puree
2 large eggs
1 large egg yolk
¼ cup granulated sugar
1½ teaspoons ground cinnamon
⅛ teaspoon ground cloves
Pinch of kosher salt
1⅓ cups whole milk
8 slices good-quality white bread
Softened butter, for the griddle
Maple syrup, warmed, for serving

1 Preheat the oven to 350°F.

2 Spread the pecans out in a single layer on a pie plate and toast until fragrant and golden, 8 to 10 minutes. Let cool, then coarsely chop.

3 In a small bowl, using a wooden spoon, beat the cream cheese until smooth. Add the confectioners' sugar and beat to combine.

4 In a large bowl, whisk the pumpkin puree together with the eggs, egg yolk, granulated sugar, cinnamon, cloves, and salt. Whisk in the milk.

5 Arrange the bread in pairs and spread 4 slices with the cream cheese mixture, leaving a 1-inch border all around. Top with the other 4 slices and dip each "sandwich" into the pumpkin custard, allowing it to soak for 15 to 20 seconds. Lift the sandwiches from the custard, allowing the excess to drip back into the bowl, then place them on a platter while the griddle preheats.

6 Heat a griddle or a nonstick skillet over medium heat and generously brush with the softened butter. Add the sandwiches and cook until browned but not cooked through, turning once, about 4 minutes. Brush the skillet with butter as needed.

7 Sprinkle the almost-done French toast with confectioners' sugar, flip so the sugared side is down, and cook just until glossy, about 15 seconds. Sprinkle the top with confectioners' sugar and repeat to cook the second side. Transfer the French toast to a baking sheet and finish cooking in the oven until just firm and the edges are dry, about 5 minutes. Serve the French toast with warmed maple syrup and toasted pecans and dusted with confectioners' sugar.

MARIONBERRY PANCAKES

ACTIVE: 30 MINUTES ★ TOTAL: 30 MINUTES ★
SERVES 6 (24 PANCAKES)

PANCAKES

1½ cups all-purpose flour
¼ cup stone-ground cornmeal
2 teaspoons baking powder
1 teaspoon kosher salt
3 large eggs, separated
1¼ cups whole milk
½ cup (about 6 ounces) ricotta cheese
¼ cup plus 1 tablespoon sugar
Scant ½ teaspoon grated lemon zest
Butter, for the griddle

MARIONBERRY COMPOTE

3 cups marionberries or blackberries if
    you simply can't get your hands on
    marionberries, plus more for garnish
½ teaspoon grated lemon zest
¼ cup sugar

1 Make the pancakes: In a small bowl,
whisk together the flour, cornmeal, baking
powder, and salt.

2 In a large bowl, whisk together the egg
yolks, milk, ricotta, ¼ cup of the sugar,
and the lemon zest until combined. Add the
flour mixture and whisk until smooth.

3 In another bowl, using a handheld electric
mixer, beat the egg whites on medium
speed until frothy. Increase the speed and
beat on high until soft peaks form. Beat in
the remaining 1 tablespoon of sugar. Fold
the egg whites into the batter, using a rubber
spatula, until no streaks remain.

4 Make the compote: In a medium
saucepan, combine the berries with the
lemon zest, sugar, and ½ cup of water and
bring to a boil. Simmer over moderately low
heat, stirring and crushing occasionally,
until slightly thickened, about 10 minutes.
Set aside.

5 Preheat the oven to 225°F. Preheat a
griddle over medium-low heat.

6 Lightly butter the griddle and ladle a
scant ¼ cup of batter onto the griddle for
each pancake, being sure to leave enough
space between them. Cook over medium-low
heat until the pancake bottoms are golden
and their surface is just beginning to set, 1
to 2 minutes. Flip the pancakes and cook
until fluffy, golden, and cooked through,
about 1 minute longer. Transfer to plates,
keeping the pancakes warm in a low oven as
you continue cooking the rest, buttering the
griddle between batches.

7 Serve the pancakes topped with the berry
compote.

Make ahead: The compote and batter
can be refrigerated separately overnight.
Whisk the batter gently if it has separated
slightly and bring the compote to room
temperature before serving.

BIRD IN A GRILLED CHEESE NEST

TOTAL: 25 MINUTES ★ MAKES 2 SANDWICHES

4 slices best-quality packaged white sandwich bread

2 tablespoons mayonnaise (not reduced fat)

2 tablespoons freshly grated Parmigiano-Reggiano

3 ounces (about 1 cup) coarsely shredded cheese, such as fontina, unaged Asiago, or unaged Gouda

1 scallion, thinly sliced

Unsalted butter, for the pan

2 large eggs

Truffle salt (optional)

1 Preheat the broiler, setting the rack 6 inches from the heat.

2 Arrange the bread on a work surface and spread 1 side only with the mayonnaise, evenly and to the edges. Sprinkle the Parmesan over the mayonnaise and press lightly to make it adhere. Flip the bread and add the coarsely shredded cheese and the scallions to 2 of the slices. Close the sandwiches, with the Parmesan-encrusted sides out.

3 Heat an ovenproof griddle or skillet over medium heat and lightly grease with butter. Add the sandwiches and cook over moderate heat until lightly browned on the bottom, 1 to 1½ minutes.

4 Transfer the sandwiches to a cutting board. Using a biscuit cutter or the rim of a glass, cut out a 2-inch hole in the center of each sandwich. Return the sandwiches and cutouts to the griddle, browned side up, and melt a sliver of butter in the holes. Crack an egg into each hole and cook over medium heat for about 30 seconds. Transfer the griddle to the broiler and cook until the top is browned and the egg whites are just set but the yolk is still runny, about 2 minutes. The tops and bottoms should be perfectly golden, but be careful not to overtoast the bread.

5 Sprinkle the eggs with truffle salt, if using, and serve immediately, with the cutouts of bread on the side.

FRIED EGG SANDWICH WITH SAUTÉED GREENS AND SAUSAGE

TOTAL: 20 MINUTES ★ MAKES 4 SANDWICHES

1 tablespoon unsalted butter

4 ounces pork sausage, such as Jimmy Dean's premium pork sausage

1 medium yellow onion, halved and thinly sliced

6 cups (packed—about 5 ounces) chopped, stemmed greens, such as kale, collards, or mustard greens

½ teaspoon chopped fresh rosemary

¼ teaspoon kosher salt

¼ teaspoon freshly ground black pepper

½ cup low-sodium chicken broth

1 tablespoon cider vinegar

2 tablespoons extra-virgin olive oil

4 large eggs

4 multigrain English muffins, split and toasted

1 small garlic clove, peeled

1 In a large skillet set over medium heat, melt the butter, then add the sausage and cook, breaking up the meat into small lumps, until crisp and browned, about 4 minutes. Add the onion, cover, and cook, stirring occasionally, until softened, about 5 minutes. Uncover and cook, stirring, until lightly golden, about 5 minutes longer.

2 Stir in the greens and rosemary and season with salt and pepper to taste. Add the broth and vinegar, cover, and cook over medium heat, stirring occasionally, until wilted and tender, about 8 minutes. Uncover the pan and cook until the liquid is evaporated, about 2 minutes longer. Keep warm.

3 In a separate large nonstick skillet, heat 1 tablespoon of the oil over medium heat. Add the eggs, cover, and cook for 2 minutes. Flip and cook 30 seconds longer.

4 Brush the toasted English muffins with the remaining 1 tablespoon of oil and rub lightly with the garlic clove to impart flavor. Mound the greens on the bottom halves of the muffins and top with an egg. Close the sandwiches and serve right away.

RED FLANNEL HASH WITH POACHED EGGS, SMOKED SALMON, AND HORSERADISH

ACTIVE: 30 MINUTES ★ TOTAL: 1½ HOURS ★
SERVES 4

1 bunch baby beets, 1½ to 2 inches in diameter (about 4), scrubbed

1 sprig of fresh thyme

Kosher salt and freshly ground black pepper

¾ pound fingerling potatoes, scrubbed

2 tablespoons unsalted butter

1 tablespoon vegetable oil

1 small onion, finely chopped

1 garlic clove, minced

4 ounces sliced smoked salmon

1 to 2 tablespoons prepared horseradish, squeezed dry

1 tablespoon chopped fresh dill, plus more for garnish

4 large eggs

Hot sauce, for serving

1 Preheat the oven to 350°F.

2 In a small baking dish, combine the raw beets with the thyme and ¼ cup of water and season with salt and pepper to taste. Cover with foil and roast until tender (a knife easily pierces the beets), about 45 minutes. Let cool completely, then peel the beets and cut into ¾-inch pieces.

3 Meanwhile bring a medium saucepan of water to a boil. Add the potatoes and cook until tender, about 10 minutes. Drain and pat them dry, then cut them into ¾-inch pieces.

4 In a large skillet, melt the butter in the oil. Add the onion and garlic and cook over medium heat, stirring occasionally, until softened, 4 to 5 minutes.

5 Add the potatoes and cook until browned in spots, 5 to 6 minutes.

6 Add the beets and cook until lightly browned, about 5 minutes longer, lightly crushing the potatoes and beets.

7 Add the salmon and cook just until heated through and firm, about 2 minutes. Stir in the horseradish and dill and season lightly with salt and pepper to taste.

8 Crack the eggs into individual ramekins, being careful not to break the yolks. Bring a deep skillet of water to a boil and season with salt. Reduce the heat to low and one by one pour the eggs into the simmering water, spacing the eggs evenly. Poach the eggs until the whites are set but the yolks are still runny, about 3 minutes. Using a slotted spoon, transfer the eggs to a paper towel–lined plate and gently pat dry.

9 Spoon the salmon hash onto plates and top each with a poached egg. Garnish with dill and serve right away; pass the hot sauce at the table.

MANY-GRAIN GRANOLA

ACTIVE: 15 MINUTES ★ TOTAL: 1 HOUR ★
MAKES ABOUT 8 CUPS

3 tablespoons unsalted butter, plus more
    for the pan

⅓ cup maple syrup

3 tablespoons canola oil

¼ cup (packed) light brown sugar

½ teaspoon ground cinnamon

½ teaspoon kosher salt

Pinch of baking soda

2 cups old-fashioned rolled oats (preferably
    thick cut)

1 cup kamut, spelt, or quinoa flakes
    (or 1 additional cup of rolled oats)

1 cup raw slivered almonds

¼ cup golden flax seed meal (or seeds ground
    in a coffee grinder)

½ tablespoon chia seeds (optional)

½ cup dried cranberries

½ cup golden raisins

½ cup dried sour cherries, chopped

1 Preheat the oven to 300°F. Butter a large rimmed baking sheet.

2 In a large microwave-safe bowl, combine the butter, maple syrup, oil, and brown sugar and microwave on high for 30 seconds. Add the cinnamon, salt, and baking soda and whisk until smooth. Add the oats, kamut, almonds, flax, and chia seeds, if using, and stir until completely coated.

3 Spread out the mixture on the baking sheet and bake in the center of the oven, stirring occasionally, until golden, toasted, and fragrant, about 40 minutes.

4 Let cool completely, then add the cranberries, raisins, and cherries. Store the granola in an airtight container at room temperature for up to 2 weeks.

Kath and Dave

BEATING THE BRUNCH LINE

KATH and DAVE ALERT! Joking, but yes: we are back. Just thought we'd swing by for a quick tip about breakfast for all of you eaters out there. A lot of idiots here in Portland waste their time waiting in line for brunch. They wait for *hours*! Then it takes them another hour to pick out the right table; then they order a slow-cooked egg, which takes another hour. It's one big joke. We are laughing out loud. The whole point of breakfast is that it should be *quick*. IN and OUT. Chow it down, and start your day.

We've got the brunch line *beat* with one easy solution: our big bag of granola we carry around. We just carry around the granola in a big plastic zip-bag and kick off our day with a handful or two. If we are hungry a few minutes later, we just dip in the bag for another handful. Just try to make this granola at home, and you'll see how easy it is. You make it, and then you can keep dipping for handfuls until you're full. But meanwhile you can do other things, like organize the garage, go on a hike, or go to the grocery store to buy more granola supplies.

Once you try this granola, you'll never have to go to brunch ever again. You'll thank us, and in advance we say: *We Knew It* and *You're Welcome.*

CUP OF JOE SIDE OF DOUGH

ACTIVE: 20 MINUTES ★ TOTAL: 1 HOUR ★
MAKES 16 SIDES OF DOUGH

2 cups all-purpose flour

¼ cup granulated sugar

1 tablespoon baking powder

½ teaspoon kosher salt

Pinch of ground nutmeg

1 stick (¼ pound, or 8 tablespoons) unsalted butter, cubed and chilled, plus 2 teaspoons unsalted butter, softened

1 cup heavy cream

1 large firm, just-ripe banana, cut into ¼-inch rounds

½ cup Nutella

1 large egg yolk mixed with 1 tablespoon heavy cream (or milk)

Coarse sugar, for sprinkling

1 Preheat the oven to 375°F. Line a large baking sheet with parchment paper.

2 In a food processor, combine the flour with 3 tablespoons of the granulated sugar, the baking powder, the salt, and the nutmeg.

3 Add the 8 tablespoons of chilled butter and pulse until the butter is the size of small peas. Lift the lid and drizzle the 1 cup of cream all over. Pulse several times just until moistened.

4 Turn the mixture out onto a floured work surface and knead very briefly until the dough comes together. On a floured surface, roll the dough to a 16 × 7 × ¼-inch-thick rectangle. Transfer the dough to the prepared baking sheet and refrigerate until chilled, 30 minutes.

MY SECRET BRUNCH SPOT

Mr. Mayor here. Fred and Carrie asked me to tell you about the place to go for Cup of Joe Side of Dough. Unfortunately, I'm not going to. I just can't afford to let the word get out about the place that serves it. I go there every Sunday morning and there's an open booth waiting for me. I have so much to attend to keep the City of Portland in good shape, and I can't afford to wait in line for breakfast on my Sunday mornings. I genuinely apologize, but there are few things I keep to myself and this is one of them.

I did, however, manage to convince Ed to share the recipe for his prized Cup of Joe Side of Dough. So at least you can try it out by making it at home. Again, I would like to formally apologize to you for my secrecy. And I apologize to Fred and Carrie. And I ask Fred and Carrie not to tell anyone about my secret place. Thank you.

5 Meanwhile, in a medium nonstick skillet, melt the remaining 2 teaspoons of butter over medium heat. Using a pastry brush, brush a tiny bit of the butter onto a small plate.

6 In a small bowl, toss the bananas with the remaining 1 tablespoon of granulated sugar. Add the bananas to the skillet and cook over high heat, turning once, until caramelized but not mushy, about 1 minute. Transfer to the buttered plate and let cool.

7 Spread the Nutella evenly onto the dough, leaving a ½-inch border along the long sides. Arrange the cooled bananas over the Nutella and roll the dough tightly into a long cylinder.

8 Brush the dough cylinder with the egg yolk–cream mixture and dust liberally with the coarse sugar. Cut the dough into 8 equal stubby cylinders. Cut each piece diagonally in half to make somewhat triangle-shaped pieces of dough and arrange them on the prepared baking sheet, sugared side up.

9 Lightly press the scones on an angle to show the Nutella spiral, slightly. Bake the scones in the center of the oven for 22 minutes, until deeply golden, rotating the pan from front to back for even cooking. Let cool slightly, then serve warm or at room temperature.

Make ahead: The scones can be stored in an airtight container at room temperature for up to 4 days. Rewarm them before serving.

ALIKI FARM EGGS BAKED OVER ALIKI FARM VEGETABLES

ACTIVE: 30 MINUTES ★ TOTAL: 40 MINUTES ★
SERVES 2

½ **lemon**

6 **baby artichokes**

½ **pound thin asparagus, trimmed and cut into 2-inch lengths**

4 **scallions, cut into 2-inch lengths, bulbs halved lengthwise**

2 **tablespoons unsalted butter**

2 **tablespoons extra-virgin olive oil**

¼ **teaspoon chopped fresh thyme**

Kosher salt and freshly ground black pepper

½ **cup low-sodium chicken broth**

2 **large eggs**

1 Preheat the oven to 400°F.

2 Fill a bowl with water and squeeze the lemon into it, then add the lemon half. Pluck off and discard the outer leaves of the artichokes, revealing a yellow-green core. Using a serrated knife, trim off the top one-third of the artichoke. Cut into 4 or 5 slices, lengthwise, and add to the lemon water to prevent oxidizing. Repeat with the remaining artichokes.

3 Bring a medium saucepan of water to a boil and line 3 small plates with paper towels. Drain the artichokes and add them to the boiling water. Blanch them for 2 minutes; then, using a slotted spoon or an Asian spider strainer, transfer them to a paper towel–lined plate to drain. Blanch the asparagus pieces for 1 minute, then transfer them to another paper towel–lined plate. Blanch the scallions just until wilted, about 30 seconds, then transfer them to the third paper towel–lined plate. Pat all the vegetables dry.

4 In a large nonstick skillet, melt the butter in the oil. Add the artichokes and thyme and season with salt and pepper to taste. Cook over medium-high heat, stirring once or twice, until golden, about 4 minutes. Add the asparagus and scallions and cook until crisp-tender, about 4 minutes longer. Add the broth and bring to a boil.

5 Divide the mixture between 2 individual baking dishes and make a well in the center. Crack an egg into the well and season with salt and pepper. Bake until the whites are set but the yolk is still runny, 7 to 8 minutes. Serve right away.

urthermore then, I beseech you: tend to thy barnyard with many and diverse seeds, so ye would abound more and more thy plants yielding good seed. Bring forth thy Farm-Fresh Eggs, lain in My fields, born from the pleasant plants, and, in turn, you shall have them for food. Which of you shall have a lover and which a Kingdom? Who among you will wander through the alfalfa and then trip and accidentally fall into a nearby well and then rise in a garment, not of linen but of cloth? Then in the fifth year upon my death, do not ask me to stay. I gotta go. Tell me to go. Thank you. I wanted to say goodbye to You and it means a lot to me. That You would tell me that I should Go.

Aliki 8:12-6

ACKNOWLEDGMENTS

We would like to thank the City of Portland, our Editors, Recipe Producers, Taste Testers, Local Farmers, Occasionally Regional Famers (only when we had to—but thanks, guys!), Mixologists, Neighborhood Grocers, Salt Dealers, Allergy Specialists, Mr. Mayor, our **Font Consultants** (just messing with you guys!), Members of The Green Kitchen Council, Pete the Spoon Whiddler and Sons, and of course, the people who came up with the idea to make restaurants in Portland look like old wooden and iron apothecaries. Usually with a fireplace or some alternative form of hearth. . . . And the legs of the tables seem kind of rusty, but not in a dangerous way. Sometimes there are old science diagrams on the walls. We just really love the whole aesthetic, so thank you from the bottom of our hearts for making that a reality.

–FRED, CARRIE & JONATHAN

PHOTOGRAPHY & ILLUSTRATION CREDITS

Page 1: Jim Massey (pig); **pages 2–3:** Shutterstock © filmlandscape (moss) and Rae Ann Spitzenberger (burger); iStock © dem10 (Marco); **pages 12–13:** Rae Ann Spitzenberger (map); **page 20:** iStock © Dudi-art (leopard print); **page 24:** Shutterstock © Picsfive (torn paper); **page 27:** Martha O'Leary (Garmin map); **pages 28–29:** Shutterstock © Marko Poplasen (placemat) and Alane Gianetti (Pretzel Knots illustrations); **pages 34, 36:** Rae Ann Spitzenberger (TV and chicken); **page 41:** Gabriel Levine (Message from the Mayor); **pages 42–43:** Jim Massey (hand lettering); **page 50:** Ray Spitzenberger (ant illustrations); **page 57:** Elina Nudelman (note cards); **pages 58–59:** Danielle Deschenes (Guide to Picking a Table); **page 62:** Shutterstock © David Smart (file folder); **page 63:** Jim Massey (Colin); **page 66–67, 69:** Anna Thompson (1890s butcher's parlour); **pages 70–71:** Shutterstock © Valentin Agapov (brick wall) and iStock © crossroadscreative (City of Roses logo); **pages 72–73:** Rae Ann Spitzenberger (Stu's Stews menu) and Shutterstock © POORMAN (wood frame); **page 75:** Jason Polan (background illustration); **page 86–87:** Rae Ann Spitzenberger (BYOB illustration); **page 94:** Jason Polan (background illustration); **page 97:** IFC (the rats); **pages 98–99:** Na Kim (Dumpster Divers' Dinner Party Guide); **page 100:** iStock © sumnersgraphicsinc (cardboard); **pages 110–111, 113:** Maren Childs (durian illustrations); **page 117:** iStock © nicoolay (wallpaper) and iStock © assalve (frame); **page 119:** Jason Polan (background illustration); **page 122:** iStock © KotzurYangCreative (crumbs); **pages 128–129, 130:** Martha O'Leary (celery illustrations); **page 134:** Jason Polan (background illustration); **pages 136–137:** Rae Ann Spitzenberger (map); **pages 138–139:** Shutterstock © serazetdinov (paper), Shutterstock © Norma Zaro (corkboard), Gabriel Levine (Coffee Shop Manifesto); **pages 146–147:** Shutterstock © 9nong (wood paneling), iStock © martijnmulder (tape), iStock © Lilith76 (coffee stain); **page 148–149:** Jason Polan (background illustration); **pages 150–151:** Heather Williamson (Mixologist's Guide to Ice illustrations); **page 154:** iStock © leminuit (fabric); **page 165:** Jason Polan (background illustrations); **page 169:** iStock © fmatte (scroll); **page 176:** Jessie Sayward Bright (Farmer's Market illustration).

IFC: pages 8–9: IFC/Evan Sung (Kath & Dave and Toni & Candace) and Augusta Quirk/IFC (Joaquin); **page 17:** Bryce & Lisa; **page 20:** Nina; **page 21:** Nina & Lance; **page 26:** Garmin; **pages 30–31:** Johnny and Around the World graphics; **page 32:** rock star chefs; **page 35:** Doug & Claire; **page 38:** movie theater employees; **page 40:** Spyke; **page 44:** Bryce & Lisa; **page 48:** CSA letterhead; **page 49:** Brendan & Michelle; **page 54:** Claire; **page 60:** Peter & Nance; **page 62:** chicken; **page 64:** Scott Green/IFC (Peter & Nance); **pages 72–73:** Stu and Donald; **page 76:** Augusta Quirk/IFC (Malcolm & Kris) and IFC (Fart Patio sign and Erin); **page 78:** Augusta Quirk/IFC (Malcom & Kris); **page 80:** Alexandra; **page 81:** IFC/Evan Sung (chore wheel); **page 82:** Malcolm; **page 84:** Augusta Quirk/IFC (Malcolm & Kris); **page 85:** Mr. Mayor and Bridgetown Weekly; **page 89:** Craig's Crazy Guac Tacos; **page 101, 102:** gutterpunks; **page 104:** Ellen; **page 105:** Doug & Claire; **page 109:** Nina & Lance; **page 110:** Brendan & Michelle; **page 115:** Mr. Mayor and Café Y2K; **page 116:** Augusta Quirk/IFC (Mr. Mayor); **page 121:** Doug & Claire; **page 122:** Augusta Quirk/IFC (Doug with dog); **page 123:** Lance; **page 130:** Augusta Quirk/IFC (Marty and Bloody Mary); **page 132:** coffeeland photo; **page 135:** staff favorites; **page 140:** Augusta Quirk/IFC (Nance); **pages 142:** Milk Advisory Board logo and Frank DiMarco/IFC (Milk Advisory Board photo); **page 145:** Augusta Quirk/IFC (Joaquin); **pages 146:** Megan Holmes/IFC (Gahvin); **page 154:** Fisherman's Porch logo; **page 167:** Danielle Mathias/IFC (Mr. Mayor); **page 168:** brunch special.

INDEX

-The-
Portlandia
FARMERS
MARKET

FEATURING

The Gluten
F.R.E.E
BLUEGRASS BAND

Atticus's
UNPASTEURIZED
TEMPEH
*RECENTLY
RECOGNIZED
by the
C.D.C

BEATRIX's
$5 for FIVE
Blueberries

BUY LOCAL • DON'T FORGET YOUR BAG!!!!!!!!!!!!!!

SATURDAYS 11 AM → 2 PM
~ May to November ~